SMART BUSINESS, BETTER YOU

The Entrepreneur's Guide to
Health, Wealth, and **Happiness**

DENIERO BARTOLINI

Torchbearing
House

hello@torchbearinghouse.com

ISBN: 978-1-7386518-0-1 (paperback)
ISBN: 978-1-7386518-1-8 (ebook)
ISBN: 978-1-7386518-2-5 (hardcover)
ISBN: 978-1-7386518-3-2 (audiobook)

Ordering Information:
Special discounts are available on quantity purchases by corporations, associations, and others. For details, contact us at hello@torchbearinghouse.com

CONTENTS

Section 5: Lifestyle Design

SUCCESS (noun)

suc·cess | \ sək-'ses \

1a: degree or measure of succeeding in an endeavor

1b: the attainment of wealth, position, honors, or the like

But really: the feeling you get when you're doing exactly what you want to do at any specific time. The more you experience that feeling, the more successful you are.

CHAPTER 1

THE PROBLEM TO SOLVE

This is a book about money and freedom as much as it is about life. I won't just show you how to set up a lifestyle business but also how to become the type of person who can build and scale that lifestyle business. As an internet entrepreneur myself, I will also demystify the digital business world so you can protect yourself from the make-money-online and get-rich-quick scams that lure people in the industry by setting unrealistic expectations.

In the following chapters, I will lay out the blueprint that helped me shift from a stressed-out, burned-out solopreneur (someone who runs a business by themselves) to a happy and fulfilled CEO of a lifestyle business. Following these steps will help you launch a successful lifestyle business of your own and live a life that you've only ever dreamed of! But let me ask you something. Why have you been dreaming of this life anyway? Actually, you and I may have the same answer to this question.

I started working in corporate Canada in 2011, and by 2015, I was already fed up. I didn't understand why I had to be out of the house between 7 a.m. and 7 p.m. to make a living. Then, if you count the time that it takes to shop for groceries, cook, eat your meals, go to the gym, and complete a basic self-care routine, I had a 30-minute window of free time left. On a good day, I'd manage to go to bed on time and sleep seven hours, but most of the time, I'd stay up late, lose sleep, and systematically start the following day with a headache. What a crazy cycle!

The only thing that made me feel better was that I knew I wasn't alone. The story I just told you describes the average professional or solopreneur. In fact, just a few years ago, if you weren't the one leading that crazy lifestyle, you certainly knew someone who did.

It didn't matter if you were a lawyer, an accountant, a salesperson, or a small-business owner. Working long hours and being proud of doing so were the norm, and in general, people didn't think anything of it.

But if you look at this pattern more closely, you'll see there's a good reason why things can run that way for so many years.

If you live in a big city, for example, your living expenses are higher than average, forcing you to work harder to make more money and advance your career. And in a world where most people trade time for money, it's only a matter of time until the race for "most hours worked" becomes unsustainable.

For those stuck in the time-for-money paradigm, being away from family and friends is simply the price to pay for being able to afford nice, comfortable things. The good car, the cozy home, and the fancy watch are the treats you get to nibble on while working long hours away from the people you care about the most.

That's what a lack of awareness will do to you. If you don't find a way to earn good money without sacrificing time and relationships, you'll just end up doing what everyone else does. And you'll spend years overworking yourself to the brink of a nervous breakdown while being hooked on that basic comfort level that you convinced yourself you enjoy.

It's like the story of the old dog sitting on a rusty nail and howling all day. The nail is uncomfortable enough to make the dog whine, but not painful enough to make it move to find another spot.

But realistically, before communication and collaboration tech became mainstream, building a remote and automated business was not an easy feat. Sure, the tools have been there for quite some time, but the collective mentality hadn't yet caught up with the times.

Think about Zoom. I used to use it for my sales calls and coaching meetings back in 2016, but I'd always receive pushback from my prospects. I was already using screen-sharing technology in sales in 2012, but more often than not, I'd hear people mutter under their breath things like "I hope this is not a scam."

For those already working in tech and in a select few other industries, the transition to remote working, even before the pandemic, was easier and more natural. But for anyone else, the change seemed just too impractical.

Why would you give up your office space and stop seeing your clients in person?

Why would you try to figure out how to stay productive while working from home?

Why would you try to convince your customers that you are still operating at full capacity, even though you are working remotely?

Why would you quit your full-time corporate job and try to reinvent the wheel?

Those are not easy things to do. No matter how stressed-out or burned-out someone is, most people would rather keep living according to the status quo instead of taking risks like those above.

The Tech Tipping Point

Between 2017 and 2020, a series of events triggered the biggest cultural shift the world has seen since the last industrial revolution. Broadband internet became widely available, making long-distance communication and collaborative work far easier. Hardware and software became so user friendly that even the most tech-illiterate individuals adopted it. And then COVID-19 came along, and the world was forced to reimagine every activity we were used to doing.

In less than five years, we underwent a digital makeover that affected all aspects of our lives. From working, hanging out with friends, and exercising, to buying groceries and ordering dinner, we adopted the digital alternatives to these in-person activities.

Don't worry—I'm not here to tell you that hanging out with your friends over Zoom is better than meeting them in person. But when people became aware of the alternatives, they started to question useless commutes, long hours in the office, and overpriced downtown real estate.

Big corporations went fully remote and realized they could save millions of dollars in overhead costs. Professionals started operating from home and gained back hours every day by ditching lengthy commutes. Solopreneurs and small-business owners learned to tap into a much broader market than their local area once they went online. Restaurants found new ways to serve their clients and came up with new business models from scratch.

Take food delivery, for example. Ten years ago, buying food through an app was unheard of, but now food-delivery services—both for groceries and restaurant meals—have become must-have apps.

And what about workout gear like Peloton bikes or Aviron rowing machines? These went from being niche workout equipment for die-hard fitness junkies to becoming staples of any respectable home gym.

We can say the same thing for virtual reality (VR). Just a few years ago, VR was nothing more than a buzzword. If you wanted to experience virtual reality, you either had to go to a VR arcade—there was only one in the Greater Toronto Area, a city with over six million people—or wait for a technology fair and look for a VR booth. But in 2021, sales of VR headsets like the Oculus Quest 2 have surpassed Xbox sales.

And, of course, let's not forget e-commerce! A study from the market research company eMarketer shows that e-commerce sales will make up 22.3 percent of total retail sales by 2023.[1]

Humans are inherently lazy and will resist change if given a choice. But when change becomes the new normal, something remarkable happens to those who are left behind. The rusty nail becomes painful enough that even the old dog stands up and starts looking for a better solution.

---

[1] Sara Lebow, "Worldwide Ecommerce Continues Double-Digit Growth Following Pandemic Push to Online," Insider Intelligence, August 19, 2021, https://www.emarketer.com/content/worldwide-ecommerce-continues-double-digit-growth-following-pandemic-push-online.

I've worked with countless lifestyle entrepreneurs from dozens of countries over the past 10 years, and while I've seen radically different business models and levels of success, all the business owners who took the leap say the same thing: There's more to life than making money by sacrificing health and relationships. You *can* have your cake and eat it too. You don't have to follow the herd. You are in control of your destiny, and if you want to change your life, you have the tools to make it all happen. There's never been a better time to run a lifestyle business.

New entrepreneurs are starting to realize that everyone, including their employees and customers, are looking for new standards. Whether it's flexible hours, easier access to services, more buying options, or location freedom, these perks go far beyond low prices or good pay with benefits.

So if you are about to scale a lifestyle business, your goal should be to incorporate these new preferences in your company. That way, the upsides are twofold. First, you will make your team happier, serve more people, and grow your business faster. And second, you'll have more time to spend with those you love while doing things that make you happy.

But what if you are a professional? Maybe you are an accountant, a lawyer, or a doctor. You spent years getting your degrees and postgrad certificates. You finally entered the workforce and thought that you would either climb the corporate ladder or advance your career as a freelancer. But now that the rules of business have changed, what does it all mean for you? Should you discard all the hard work you've done over the years and build a lifestyle business? Or should you keep doing everything as you have been doing it so far? The answer lies right in between the two.

Most successful entrepreneurs I had the pleasure to work with or interview on my podcast took this approach. They first spent some time analyzing their skills and the value they provided to their markets. Then they designed a few solutions that would allow them to thrive with a remote business model. Some of these ideas called for a complete remote setup, while others allowed them to create hybrid companies.

So, let's look at both options.

1. Fully Remote

"If you moved across the globe today, could your business survive?" That's the first question I ask all my coaching clients, and that is the easiest test you can run to see if your company qualifies for a chance at becoming an actual lifestyle business.

As a rule of thumb, businesses that can go fully remote include the following:

- Digital service providers (ad agencies, graphic designers, video editors, web developers, copywriters, etc.)

- Accountants

- Some types of lawyers

- Coaches and consultants

- E-commerce entrepreneurs

- Personal trainers and fitness instructors

- Professions that don't require you to meet clients in person

2. Hybrid, Remote, or In Person

But what if you are someone like a dentist or a massage therapist? You need to be where your clients are. So, how can you create a remote business?

This scenario requires more thinking, but I assure you that once you crack the code of leveraging the remote-work aspect, your business will grow faster and enjoy much healthier profit margins. Here are a couple of basic examples.

As a lawyer, you could hire a remote ad specialist to get you leads and a remote sales rep to close deals. That way, you can service more clients, use the extra space in your studio to hire an additional lawyer, and scale up from there.

Or, as a yoga studio owner, you could outsource all the sales and admin work to remote team members, downsize your studio, and save money on rent. You can then use that extra cash to run ads and offer more classes every day, or you can pay yourself better.

Think out of the box. No matter what your niche and offer are, keep in mind that you can combine in-person and online services as you please.

What if you are a physiotherapist? You could still offer in-person sessions two days a week and then create an online program that people can buy to solve a specific problem (e.g., an eight-week back-pain relief boot camp).

The same goes for almost any profession. As a dentist, you could see patients a couple of times a week and then create a secondary stream of income by using your skills and making it totally remote (e.g., dental practice consulting). After all, we live in the information age, and people will pay for your knowledge.

The (Un)bearable Pain

As you can see, there are plenty of ways you can start and scale your business remotely, yet the vast majority of people who read this book will keep on doing the same old things they did before and achieving the same mediocre results.

People tend to avoid consciously exposing themselves to the unknown. Instead, they retreat into their comfort zones, which are often filled with anxiety, stress, and possibly even depression.

Our society has normalized discontent, and this has to stop. Have you ever found yourself with a group of people and felt awkward talking about your success stories because everyone else was only complaining about their lives?

It almost seems that, to be a functioning, bona fide adult, you need to be upset or annoyed about something. And, conversely, if you are constantly positive and look forward to advancing in life, you must be naive or immature.

It's crazy! This addiction to complaining is what keeps the masses stagnant.

In all fairness, most people who complain without taking action have been programmed since birth to believe that they don't have control over their circumstances. This creates a series of totally irrational fears, which are then used as excuses for their inaction.

The most common fear is the fear of failure.

"What if I don't achieve the goal?" If you read that question a couple of times, you can see that it's not logical. The only way you won't achieve your goal for sure is by not getting started! Yet, most people will still not go for it and will try to rationalize their inertia with this very fear.

The second is the fear of being judged by others. This is also irrational because it implies that you would rather live your entire life doing something you hate so that you can avoid being judged by someone for a very limited time.

And then there's the fear of success. This is the most well-founded fear because people know that success must not only be achieved but also maintained. Once you reach it, you need to show up every day to hold your ground. If you scale your business to multiple seven figures and hire a team, you'll be responsible for that team in the long run. If you become a world-renowned speaker and author, you will have to travel from conference to conference for years on end.

But even though the fear of success is not illogical, it's still flawed because it's missing a key element: your personal growth. The only way to achieve lasting success is by becoming the version of yourself that will attract lasting success.

Champions don't stumble on gold medals. Instead, they forge their road to success with years of personal growth and training. So next time you wonder if you could handle lasting success, know that by the time you get there, you won't be the same person you are today.

The only antidote to this spell that stops people from following their dreams is the proverbial rock bottom. You can only discard your thoughts and feelings for so long. Then, if you're lucky, the pain and the discomfort become so unbearable that you are forced to take action. But most rock bottoms are not a gradual process. Instead, they tend to be a single event that shatters your status quo.

Maybe your partner breaks up with you because they no longer want to put up with mediocrity. Maybe you end up losing the one big client you were hanging on to, and you're left with no money to pay your bills. Or maybe, like me, you'll end up at the hospital for pushing yourself too hard and working on the wrong things.

But whatever your version of rock bottom looks like, don't resist it. Instead, learn from it, embrace it, and use it as motivation to pave your road to success.

The Prison Affecting Your Loved Ones

You may wonder why I'm focusing on the negative if I preach about keeping a positive attitude. So, let me ask you some questions.

- How are you around your loved ones when you are stressed out and anxious?

- Are you able to be fully present with your friends and relatives?

- Are your mediocre results in business affecting your personal life in any way?

The truth is that when you don't feel fulfilled, you cannot give yourself fully to the people you love the most. In my years of coaching, I have heard some version of this problem more times than any other issue.

"My partner hates that I work late every day—they think I could organize my schedule better."

"My kids barely see me during the week, and then on weekends, I'm too exhausted to spend quality time with them."

"I haven't been able to find true love because I'm always thinking about work, and it turns off everyone I get close to."

All of a sudden, when you compare a one-time rock-bottom event to a lifetime of stress and halfhearted relationships, the first option seems like a no-brainer. At least when you can't go any lower, you get to push yourself up and out of the slump.

But here's some great news. You don't have to wait passively for something terrible to happen. You can manufacture your rock bottom by raising your standards. Remember that we make our own reality. Take two people who are going skydiving, for example. The first has been looking forward to this moment for years, and she can't wait to finally jump off the plane and feel the wind on her face. The other is only doing it to make his friend happy, but he hates every second of it. They're two people doing the same thing, yet their experiences are opposites.

That's what happens when you finally raise your personal standards. You go from putting up with mediocrity to despising it. You'll stop tolerating poor outcomes, shaky relationships, lack of self-care, long unproductive days at work, or your roller-coaster income.

It all starts with a decision and some public accountability. Once you make up your mind, tell those close to you not to let you slip back into your old ways. Then, as we'll see in section 1, you'll need to forge your new mindset by constantly exposing yourself to material like this book. Don't forget that you are trying to unlearn a lifetime of poor habits and behaviors, so don't underestimate the amount of work this process will require.

And this takes me to my last word of advice in this chapter: goals worth reaching take time and effort. There are no shortcuts.

I have been fortunate to coach some fantastic action takers who built seven- and eight-figure businesses through hard work and patience.

But, once in a while, I come across some clients who pay for my coaching, work for less than two months, and immediately give up because they don't reach the goals they were hoping for.

Here's an excerpt from an email I received last year: "Deniero, I am sorry to say this, but your coaching was not effective. I filmed and posted the videos you told me about, and I even created those training presentations that we discussed on our last call. The content has been live for over four weeks, and I still haven't gotten any clients from them. I don't have time to create more content or network in person or online."

If success were as easy as posting a couple of videos online, everyone would be living their best lives.

Do yourself a favor and set the right expectations. Adopt a marathon mindset, and show up every day, not to finish the race but to take a few significant steps in the right direction.

When you detach yourself from the end result, you get to focus on the tasks at hand, and the quality of your life and work will instantly improve.

CHAPTER 2
THE ORIGIN STORY

My Humble Beginnings

I was born in Rome, Italy, in the mid-eighties. My mother worked for an insurance company, and my father worked at the airport. They both got their jobs in the late 1970s and worked for their companies for 40 years until they retired around 2018.

My parents were the perfect employees. They were always on time, even though their commutes were brutal. They rarely called in sick, and when they did, it was always for a good reason. They booked vacation time months in advance, and they would always make sure that everything was taken care of during their absences.

Growing up, we had enough money to live a fairly comfortable life. We'd take at least one trip abroad per year, courtesy of my dad's discounted airplane tickets, and we'd eat out at least every couple of weeks.

From a very young age, I was indoctrinated in the whole "go to school and find a good job" narrative. In fact, I was so absorbed by this mentality that I wasn't even aware that there were millions of people making a living with their own businesses until I was well into my teenage years.

And to be honest, I don't think that it would have mattered if I had found out earlier. I had always seen myself as an average guy with fixed abilities—smart enough to get by but not quite smart enough to stand out in class or at work.

As a student I felt disengaged, and the only reason I made it all the way through high school was because I cared more about spending time with friends than dropping out and finding a job. I grew up with two close friends, Marta and Enrico. But since Enrico and I went to school together, he and I were inseparable. We used to sit at the back of the class and whisper to each other all day long. I always wondered how he managed to get good grades while my grades coasted around average time after time. Every day after school we'd go to his house, get some homework done, and then we'd run outside until dinnertime. To everyone else I was the class clown, but Enrico saw something more in me, and that made me feel good about myself.

The only activities I was decent at were track-and-field and hurdles. But again, I just thought that I was good because I was tall and slim. It never crossed my mind that it was because of my hard work and dedication.

When I was 14 years old, a new guy joined my team, and he was a whole inch taller than me. Within a couple of months, he was winning all the races, leaving me with three silver medals and a whole lot of anger inside. That's when I convinced myself that I was destined to be forever a number two, a follower, someone in the background, or the main character's sidekick at best.

Life felt so dull from that point on. If my skills were fixed, and I had already reached my peak, and other people were better than me, I had nothing to look forward to.

There I was, a lanky teenager with glasses and severe acne trying his best to blend in with the crowd for fear of getting noticed. I could barely imagine myself getting a real job, let alone starting a business and making a real difference in the world.

As an only child, I began leaning on my friends more and more. If I wasn't out with them, I'd lock myself in my room and call them for hours on end. When we would get a busy signal from one of our friends' phones, we knew that they were likely on dial-up internet, so we'd all turn on our modems and meet in a chat room like ICQ or MSN Messenger. Enrico loved art and science, so every time he came across a new anecdote online, he'd send over links to articles and loved to discuss them with me. Little did he know that he was making me fall in love with learning—but not just any learning.

He used to tell me, "If you're curious about something, don't be afraid to ask more questions." I hated school because I didn't want to be told what I had to memorize. But this was a different story. We talked about everything under the sun, and when we did, I felt a bit smarter every time.

There was a feeling of safety that came with knowing that I was not alone. We were all in the same boat. We were all awkward teenage kids trying to fill that void.

By the time I was 16, I was spending more time on the streets than at school. I failed a year, changed schools, and started hanging out with the wrong crowd. I created a sort of alter ego. I grew a very tall mohawk, got a few piercings, and started listening to hardcore punk.

At 16, I also received a used bass guitar as a present, and I even tried to form a band. But by the end of that summer, after practicing less than five times, my buddies and I quit because "we sucked at making music." It was too hard.

My fixed mindset convinced me that the only thing I was good at was hanging out with friends, smoking, and drinking. So when I was out of the house, I doubled down on that.

The only thing that kept me from going to the point of no return was my love for my family. Bless them! They had always been there for me, but the pain of feeling helpless was too real, so I felt I had no choice but to act out.

The Move

By the end of high school, I had come to a crossroads. I could either stay in my neighborhood and go from being a dysfunctional teenager to a broken adult or turn the page entirely and start from scratch.

A clean slate sounded more promising, so I decided to pack my bags and move overseas to Toronto, Canada, where my uncle, aunt, and cousin lived and were kind enough to host me.

My last 30 days in Italy felt way too long and drawn out. I was an emotional mess. I was hyperexcited to start my new journey, but I also didn't want to leave my family and friends behind, especially my best friend Enrico, who had recently been diagnosed with melanoma and was spending most of his days between the hospital and his home.

I spent my last night in Rome with him at his house. We looked at old photos and talked about our future plans, wishing that things were different. He wanted to join the Navy, and I wanted to pursue a career in music because I loved the idea of being on stage and entertaining people for a living.

We smoked a cigarette on his patio, then I grabbed my jacket and my camera, got his mother to snap a photo of us, and walked out to my car. Before I got in, I turned around and waved a last goodbye. I had a plane to catch early in the morning.

Image 1: Me and Enrico

I couldn't believe it. I had packed all my belongings into two suitcases, and I was flying over the Atlantic to start my brand-new life. My father was born and raised in Canada, so I had been there a couple of times before. But this time, it was for good.

During the nine-hour flight, I started planning all the things I wanted to see and do in my first few weeks there. I knew I needed to get a job to keep busy and look for a potential music college.

That was the first time I witnessed the power of changing environments firsthand. Just a few days before, I had felt hopeless and stagnant, and now I was exploding with new ideas and positive energy.

When I finally landed, my uncle picked me up. As soon as I stepped out of the airport sliding doors, I took a deep breath and coughed hard. It was December in Canada, and it was -20°C (–4°F for my U.S. friends). I had never felt that cold before, but it didn't matter to me. I felt alive. We drove down the large highway toward the city. I remember staring at the tall buildings of Toronto's skyline with a huge smile on my face.

My first months in Canada were bittersweet. Within the first week, I joined an English language school and made friends with over 15 students from Germany, Mexico, Colombia, Chile, Korea, and France. With them I explored every nook and cranny of the city, from bars and clubs to markets and museums.

But on January 20, 2006, seven weeks after I had left Italy, my best friend Enrico passed away back in Rome. I heard the horrible news early one morning, and I was out of commission for a while. I couldn't fly back in time for the funeral, so I locked myself up in my room for a few days to try to make sense of it all. My aunt and uncle were so understanding that they brought me food and left me alone to process it all.

After about a week, I finally picked up all my broken pieces and got back on my feet. I went straight to a tattoo parlor and got a ship's wheel tattooed on my back in memory of my friend. Enrico had wanted to join the Navy—the only reason he hadn't been able to was that he got sick.

I had no excuses now. I was young and healthy, and I would live my life to the fullest—for him and for me. That was a big turning point. It was as if all the fears that had dictated my choices up to that moment just disappeared.

The fear of being judged by strangers was gone. The fear of not being good enough started to dissolve too. All I had left was a long bucket list and one short life to make it all happen.

Finding Myself

My uncle owned a business and invested in stocks, and since we spent a lot of time together, I started seeing myself running one as well. Eventually, I ditched the music school path and started my college journey in business administration, which consisted of long study sessions, house parties, club nights, and a whole lot of blackouts.

At times, it felt as if I were in Italy all over again, with the only difference being that I was showing up for my passions and getting work done this time.

Once I was in college, I needed a job to pay my bills, so I started working for the student union. We helped put together some great events for orientation week (a.k.a. frosh week) and organized various activities throughout that first year.

I had such a blast that by the end of the season I decided to run for director of campus life. I ended up winning the election! For the first time in my life, I felt the weight of being in charge of something. I now had to organize events for 25,000 students and coordinate a group of over 30 staff members. We had a budget of hundreds of thousands of dollars to spend on concerts, so my team and I decided to put together the most epic events our college had ever seen. That year I ended up hanging out with Lil Jon, the Fugees, LMFAO, and many other artists. I still look at photos from back then on Facebook and wonder how we made it all happen in just a few short months.

Image 2: Me and LMFAO

At the end of that year, I left the student union, but all those events made me want to go back on stage to perform. I decided to pick up music again, and I started producing house and techno with my friend Greg. We even started a podcast to keep our fans engaged. I loved music production because it gave me a reason to zone out on my computer and master a piece of software. We worked hard at our craft, and before long we started seeing some good results.

The following year, my good friend Cody, a club promoter,

wanted to create an online house-music community for Toronto, and since he and I used to host parties at my place, I helped him launch it. The Facebook group grew to 70,000 people within months, and because of it, Greg and I got to play all over the city.

Eventually, I fell out of love with the party scene, and I stopped producing music and spinning at clubs, but those formative years taught me some of the greatest life lessons. I could make a living doing what I loved. Now I just needed to find my true calling.

After graduating, I struggled to find a job in marketing, so I took a job as an inside-sales rep for a start-up in Toronto. Back then, tech start-ups were popping up on every corner and getting a sales job was as easy as applying and passing one interview. I loved the energy and the culture of the tech world, and the free meals and transportation that we got as benefits made the deal even sweeter.

But since I was in it for the money, when another sales opportunity popped up, this time with better pay and commission, I immediately resigned and started a new job selling pay-per-click ads to small businesses across Canada. We had to cold-call hundreds of numbers a day and try to convince our prospects to pay us between $750 and $2,500 a month to be featured on the first page of Google for their respective services.

The large sales floor with 150 people felt like a high school cafeteria. We had teams of 15 reps, and everyone knew each other. At lunch, people would mingle in groups, play foosball, pool, or go for a walk around the block. Most of us were just starting out in our careers, but we were already feeling burned out due to long hours in the office (12 or more each day) and our poor eating and sleeping habits.

I wouldn't say I loved the job, but I made some great friends and learned a few valuable lessons, the most important being deliberate practice. We'd spend hours every week mastering our script, from training our tone and inflection to closing deals on the spot. Each week we'd listen to our calls and pick apart a specific area that needed work. Nothing was left to chance. If something wasn't perfect, we'd isolate it and practice it until we mastered it.

Our managers would ask, "Now that you listened to your call again, what would you have done differently?" Then we'd break into smaller groups and practice, practice, practice. This system was so effective that to this day I use the same sales training technique in my coaching programs and with my sales reps at The Remote CEO.

After about five years in inside sales, I was ripe with experience but still broke and unmotivated, and worst of all, I had no idea why. I was putting in the hours, but I felt as if I had reached the ceiling. So I took action and asked to change departments, and that's when I started my digital marketing career.

I went from cold-calling and running sales presentations to taking care of 25 Shopify and Facebook ad accounts. I could see the similarities between being a music producer and an internet marketer. They both required me to use deep focus and master software. So, although this was not a commission role, I immediately felt excited and challenged again.

But a year after I made the switch, the company underwent a significant shift in focus and let go of about 1,500 people, including me.

I had no idea it was coming, so at first, I felt betrayed and lost. I drove my car home in a daze thinking about my parents and how much they wanted me to have a stable job. However, this experience made me see that I was done with chasing someone else's dream.

After wallowing in the disappointment of losing my job, it didn't take long for me to realize that I finally had the skills to make a go of it on my own.

Having been forced off the hamster wheel, I had a lot more time to sit at home and think. And it was during one of those thinking sessions that it all finally clicked: the reason my income hadn't increased over time was because I was chasing money instead of providing value.

When I was working in sales, I had no interest in being of service to people. All I had in mind was my commission check. So, instead of persevering in the face of adversity, I would slow down and lose focus every time I had a bad day. When people didn't pick up the phone, I'd get frustrated. When they didn't buy, I'd complain about them to my peers but forget to follow up. Money alone was not a good enough motivator.

But now things were different. I was finally confident that I could change lives with the work I did.

My Prison

I immediately started working on the creative side of my business before I went about contacting potential clients and closing deals. I spent days looking for a good name and logo—I called my agency Gold Rush Social. Once it was all set, I made a few phone calls and ended up closing my first two clients.

I couldn't believe it! I was making money working from home. It wasn't much, but it was enough to pay my bills and buy myself more time to get additional work.

I was jumping up and down in my living room like a wild man, screaming, "No more commutes! No more useless meetings! No more full days out of the house! I am set!"

But I was only half-right. Sure, from that day on I never sat in rush-hour traffic, but I was far from being set.

Within days, however, I had fallen into the trap of my old conditioning and started wasting precious time on meaningless distractions. This time I wasn't hanging out on the streets but on my couch. Thankfully this relapse didn't last long, but it was enough to make me lose momentum.

Months went by, and I still hadn't closed more deals. My initial excitement was fading, and it left behind a trail of fear and second thoughts. I would soon be getting married, and if I didn't pull my act together, my mistakes were not only going to affect me, but also my wife and my future kids.

"Why would people choose to work with me instead of a reputable big agency?"

"Could the problem be that I am charging too much for my services?"

My doubts kept on piling up, and soon I started acting with a scarcity mindset. I sounded desperate on the phone, and while the desperation made me call more people, I started selling more labor-intensive services for less money.

How labor intensive, you ask? Let's have a quick look.

Content creation (30 monthly Instagram posts), Google Ads management, Facebook Ads management, e-commerce store up-keep and management, and graphic design for $499 a month.

It didn't take long for me to hit my first $10,000 month, but at what cost?

I worked 16 hours a day and had little to no margin to hire outside help. When I did try to hire a virtual assistant, I had no time to train them or manage them, so I'd end up redoing the work myself.

Over the next couple of months, I started a cycle of late nights and large coffees to keep the ball rolling. Then, one day I was at the gym in my condo, and my chest started feeling very tight. My vision became blurry, and all of a sudden I felt weak and light-headed. I felt a small crack in my chest, and I dropped to the ground. I had no idea what to do. For the first time in my life, I thought I was going to die. All I could think was "Is this what a heart attack feels like?" In the next few minutes, I managed to make it to my apartment and my then-fiancée drove me to Toronto Western Hospital, which became my home for the next few days.

The doctor made it clear: I needed time to reset my body and mind. I was forced to take a six-week break to get back on my feet. When I was done, I had lost 75 percent of my clients. But like any obstacle, this, too, came with a couple of lessons that shaped my life and business:

- Do not trade your time for money—unless you are getting paid a ridiculous amount for it.

- Building a reputation in your niche is the key to commanding higher prices and closing better clients.

These lessons were not obvious at the beginning, though. I first had to watch my clients cancel one by one while I was sick at home. I had to go through the pain of seeing the fruits of my hard work vanish right before my eyes.

So, between naps and my next dose of meds, I started to soak up as much content about reputation building, remote team-building, and high-ticket sales as I could.

In a matter of days, I had created a plan to overcome all the issues that had forced me to retreat on my first try.

To build my brand, I started a podcast to talk about the struggles and the success stories of solopreneurs like myself. I already had podcasting experience from when I was a DJ, so it made the most sense.

I also started a personal brand page on Instagram where I shared my favorite nonfiction books and more business and personal growth content.

To feel secure about charging more and sounding more confident in my sales, I started collecting as many testimonials as possible from my successful clients.

So that I could work less, I learned how to build and manage a remote team, and I doubled down on my fulfillment by Amazon business to increase my passive income. That way I could focus on planning the business's next steps instead of working on keyword research and other tedious administrative tasks.

The Breakthrough

The first two months of the podcast were not easy. I struggled to find guests for the show, and when I recorded my solo episodes, I would stumble on my words and sound extra nervous. But after practicing and networking daily for a couple of months, I had my first breakthrough. As I was engaging with a follower on

Instagram, I was introduced to a booking agent who really liked my show, and he gave me the chance to interview many seven-, eight-, and nine-figure entrepreneurs.

I couldn't believe it! I finally had a great strategy to get back on my feet, and now I was even going to pick the brains of tons of highly successful entrepreneurs. Whenever I had a new interview lined up, I would spend hours researching my guest to get the most out of our time. I left nothing to chance.

When I interviewed Peter Taunton, the founder of Snap Fitness and Lift Brands, I was enchanted by his story and insights of how he built a *nine-figure empire of over 2,000 gym locations in 27 countries.* The fact that just a couple of decades earlier he was working as a clerk at a run-down gym made me feel as if anything was possible.

My interviews taught me the most critical business and life lessons: from team-building and sales to habit formation and routines. At this point I wasn't yet making any money through my podcast, but with all the golden nuggets I was collecting, I was just ecstatic I had the chance to rub shoulders with the giants in my industry.

Today, my podcast has over 500 episodes, my business employs between 15 and 20 remote team members, and I don't work more than 20 hours a week.

We've been working remotely, and except during the pandemic lockdowns, we've worked everywhere: from sailboats, beaches, and mountains to the Greek islands and almost every region in Italy.

After I had scaled my digital ads agency, I realized that my true calling was to help people build lifestyle businesses, so instead of offering done-for-you services, I decided to pivot into coaching and consulting. But this time I wasn't going for it without a mentor. That's when I started working with best-selling author and coach Craig Ballantyne to learn how to build and run my new business while juggling the old one.

My Lessons

My mentors used to say, "Don't give up—you don't know how close you are to your goal." But I didn't understand that truth until I got there myself.

Just a few months before, I had been in a hospital bed, ready to call it quits, but a voice inside me reminded me that there could be no turning back. Instead, that voice forced me to keep working. In fact, it told me that all I needed was to learn a few more lessons.

The first was about brand reputation. Building my brand was not easy, but it was the single most crucial factor that allowed me to charge more for my services. That allowed me to pay for quality employees. And that great team, in turn, helped me to build a stronger company.

But building a solid business is not only about hiring the right people. A team is a group of employees interacting with each other, so if you want to build a strong team, you need to learn how to manage people to get the best out of them.

Then, if you want to have a business that truly runs without you, you need to master your tools and automate as many processes as you can. It may be time consuming initially, but as soon as you set it all up, these systems can make the difference between running a time-vampire business and a lifestyle one.

See, every tweak that I make in my business may take from a few hours to a few weeks to implement. It may be something as simple as changing the copy on our booking page to increase the conversion rate or something as big as recording a new webinar or course. But once these tweaks are implemented, they improve our results little by little, and they compound over time.

Sure, in the beginning you may only increase your sales by 10 percent or save five minutes a week, but if you keep on building upon the systems you have, it won't be long until your business scales while you are enjoying a week away with your family.

After years of working remotely, I wouldn't trade this path for anything else in the world. I love taking off and exploring the world whenever I want. I love spending time with my family and not having to justify myself for wanting to do so. A year ago, my wife and I had our beautiful daughter, and I decided to work only three days a week. As a result, Brianne and I can spend virtually unlimited time with our baby, which means the world to us.

And what I love most about my job is that every day I get to help people realize their potential. Every time I see someone reach the same a-ha moments about their life and business, I feel as if I'm contributing to making the world a better place, one person at a time.

In the following chapters, I lay out the exact blueprint that I coach my clients on—the one that allowed me to go from a stressed-out, burned-out solopreneur to a happy and fulfilled CEO of a lifestyle business.

Let's get into it!

SECTION 1

MINDSET

CHAPTER 3

GOAL-SETTING

Start with Your Purpose

Before you get into the nuts and bolts of building a lifestyle business, you first need to fine-tune the engine that will take you to the top.

It doesn't matter how bad your conscious mind wants success and tries to work toward it. If you don't first change your mindset and how your subconscious mind sees yourself, you will always get the same results. Some days you'll do a bit better, but as soon as you start picking up speed, make no mistake that you will find a way to sabotage yourself.

If you are still not sure what your purpose is, let's first make a couple of things clear:

- Purpose is not about money. Money is just a by-product of your business and the service that you render through it. Therefore, the more value you provide, the more money you make.

- Purpose is not a goal. Goals are inherently time-bound.

They have a beginning, a middle, and an end. But your purpose is an ideal that you build upon every day until your last breath.

There are many ways you could build a successful business and make lots of money, but I bet you would hate waking up in the morning to work on most of them. That's why most fitness entrepreneurs wouldn't drop everything to work on Wall Street, and most bankers wouldn't quit their job to open a gym.

But when you find out your purpose, everything that looked like hard work before will turn into a game to master.

The good news for me is that most people I coach already operate with a general purpose in mind but are not sure how to narrow in on what they really want.

So, to get some clarity, you need to ask yourself a couple of questions:

1. Income aside, am I generally excited and engaged when working on my current business?

2. If not, what would get me excited to wake up in the morning?

If you don't know where to start looking, here's a big tip: Think of something that provides real value. Humans are wired to cooperate and help each other, so it's going to be much easier if your work aligns with the greater good.

I want to be clear, though: This doesn't mean that you have to change the lives of millions of people. For example, if you love to play and teach piano, you can find your purpose in helping others achieve the same level of proficiency with the instrument so that they can enjoy music as you do.

To make things easier, let me tell you mine. My purpose is to help shape the future of work, business, and society at large by empowering people to advance in life, provide value to others, and live fulfilling lives.

See, I love what I do because I was burned out and depressed like many other people just a few years ago. So as soon as I was able to use the internet to grow my business and live the lifestyle of my dreams, I couldn't wait to share my experience and influence others through my digital marketing services and coaching programs.

Before articulating my purpose, I knew that I loved working remotely and making money online. But every time my income dropped, I would automatically lose focus and drive. That's because the money was not there to motivate me. On the contrary, I would get upset because I had nothing to look forward to.

But when I worked on my purpose, and I took it upon myself to help others achieve financial and time freedom, then it all clicked.

It wasn't about the money anymore. I just wanted to show up every day and give it my best.

Think about my podcast! I only started monetizing it after my 200th episode, and still today it constitutes less than 2 percent of my income. But I still show up weekly for my listeners—sometimes even twice a week—because it's how I get to fulfill my purpose.

But I've noticed that a strange thing happens: When people listen to my show, they get to know more about me and my brands. Some of them reach out for coaching, others refer business to me, and some want my digital marketing services. People like to associate with those who have a strong purpose. Don't ever forget that.

Build Your Vision

After you discover your purpose, it's time to create a vision to help you put it into action. But before we talk about how to create that vision, let me clarify why this step is crucial.

Your vision is the long-term plan you will refer to often and use as a compass.

To make this concept easier to grasp, here's an exercise that my coaching clients love.

Let's pretend that you are a land developer, and your purpose is to create better living solutions for families that live in big cities. See, the purpose is an all-encompassing ideal, but now you need a more concrete image—a vision—to follow.

So, your vision may be to build new neighborhoods close to the city center, with lots of parks, schools, bike paths, indoor and outdoor activities, and bus and subway stops that connect these neighborhoods to the downtown core.

You may have noticed that you haven't set a specific goal yet (you will soon), but you have left the purely abstract realm of your purpose and started to ground your idea in reality.

This exercise shouldn't be challenging. Just let your imagination run wild and remember that everything is possible as long as you have the proper emotional connection to your purpose. Those intense emotions will make sure you show up every day, even when you don't feel like it.

But no matter what vision you create, make sure that it aligns with your purpose. That's the only way to ignite lasting change in your mindset and, ultimately, your behavior.

At this point, most of my clients ask me, "Deniero, how detailed does my vision need to be?"

The answer is twofold.

On the one hand, you want to bring out as much detail as possible from the vision. That's because the more images you create, the more realistic the vision will be. And since your subconscious mind doesn't know the difference between a real memory and a manufactured one, every time you recall the vision with all its great details, you will condition your subconscious to act as if your vision has already happened. In other words, you change the way you see yourself once and for all. We'll cover this in a lot more detail in chapter 4.

On the other hand, you don't want to assign deadlines at this stage. If you did the exercise correctly, your vision should be totally out of your reach for the time being. That means that you don't even know how to get to your destination. And because lots of these variables are out of your control, there's no way you can set a deadline.

The goal is to create a detailed mental picture of how it will be but be open to changing it over time. Jeff Bezos has been quoted saying, "We are stubborn on vision. We are flexible on details."[2]

Let's look at my vision so you can see what I mean. I have been working toward building a big business hub in Italy. It's an incubator where we'll help entrepreneurs and artisans leverage the

---

[2] John Greathouse, "5 Time-Tested Success Tips from Amazon Founder Jeff Bezos," *Forbes*, April 30, 2013, https://www.forbes.com/sites/johngreathouse/2013/04/30/5-time-tested-success-tips-from-amazon-founder-jeff-bezos/.

internet to grow their local brands and export their goods and services. In addition, we are going to offer grants and mentorship services. We'll also host events to promote entrepreneurship in remote areas with higher unemployment rates.

I have been working toward this vision since 2014. I have shared it several times during my interviews and magazine features, and over the years during my spare time, I try to make it as vivid as possible by imagining all its details, from the color of the floors and the height of the ceilings to the people we'll invite to speak and the types of businesses we'll help.

But because this is a vision, I don't assign a deadline to it. Because if I did, that would distract me from my current goals, like launching my group coaching program and writing this book.

Have a look at figure 1 to see how purpose, vision, and goals relate to each other.

VISION

PURPOSE

GOALS

GOALS: NARROW FOCUS ON ACTIONS AND DEADLINES

VISION: GROUNDING YOUR PURPOSE INTO REALITY

PURPOSE: THE FOUNDATION OF ALL GREAT WORK

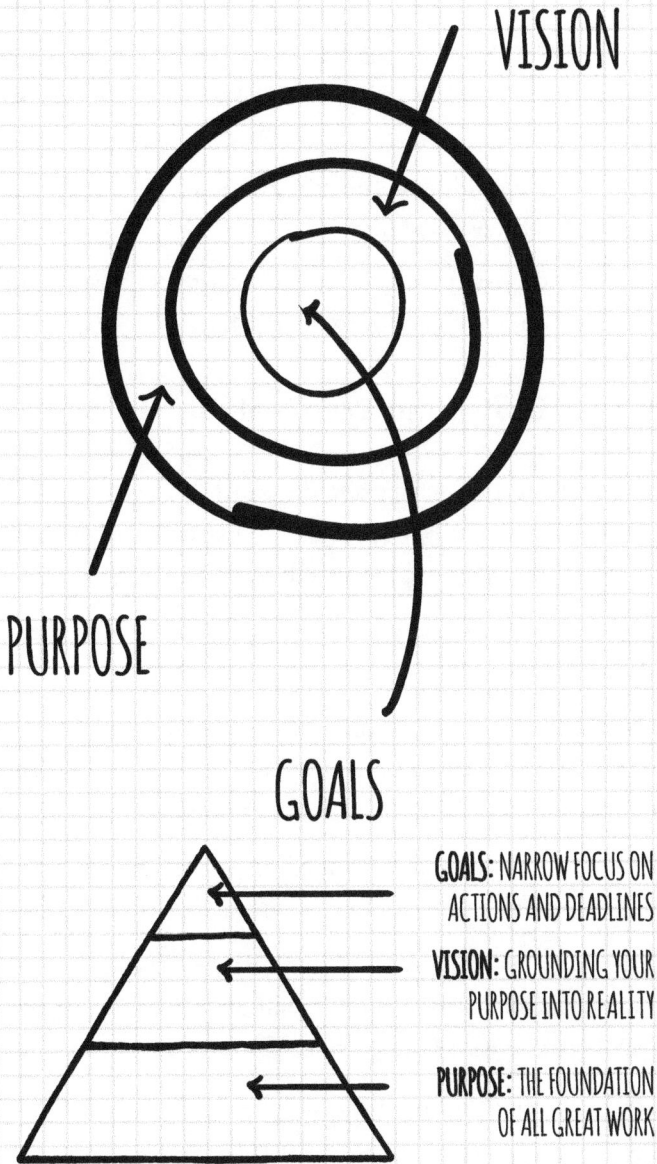

Figure 1: Purpose, Vision, and Goals

Goals are often totally within your control, and you can break them down into specific tasks and subtasks to be executed on a clear timeline. We'll come on to goal-setting soon. But, if you still don't know where to start with your vision, ask yourself these two questions:

1. Where will I be in the next 20 to 30 years, and what will my business look like?

2. Is this vision realistic, or does it stretch beyond my current knowledge and experience level?

Get Clarity Around Your Values

Before we get to goal-setting and decision-making, let's talk about values and why establishing your values is crucial if you want to be an effective leader and succeed in business.

Simply put, values are preferences, standards, and ideas that we deem essential.

If you picture your vision as the destination of a long road trip, then your values would be the rules of the road that you follow to get happily and safely to that destination.

Some values were programmed in our minds when we were young, but we also adopt or even swap values over our lifetimes.

Think about religious or cultural values. They have been ingrained in us for thousands of years, but that doesn't mean they are any better or worse than a value that you developed recently.

Here are some of my values:

1. Spending lots of time with my family

2. Practicing self-care daily

3. Refusing to get entangled in toxic relationships

4. Helping others as much as possible

5. Traveling and exploring

6. Being curious

See? Some of these values, like prioritizing family and helping others, were passed on to me by many generations, but refusing to get involved in toxic relationships and being curious are two values I created for myself after learning some compelling lessons.

As you'll see soon, these rules are there to make your life easier. One of the biggest reasons entrepreneurs fail is that they act from an emotional level instead of from a solid set of values. That causes them to make lots of incoherent choices, and they end up cannibalizing opportunity after opportunity.

You may be wondering if you are already adopting some clear values in your life, and I'll take the liberty of saying "yes." Like I said, even if you have never made a conscious effort to create them, you have already received the programming from your family and your environment.

But since your objective is to set better goals, let's equip you with more specific values so that, as long as you act with integrity, you'll never regret a decision you make along your journey.

A great question I like to ask is "What are my priorities in business and in life right now?"

You could answer, "To make a lot of money so I can buy a new investment property," or "To stop undervaluing my work," or even "To work on myself and find a great partner."

You can turn all these statements into values. And you can use these values to set goals and make better decisions (more on this in chapter 5.)

"To make a lot of money so I can buy a new investment property" becomes "Working hard and smart to provide for myself and my family."

"To stop undervaluing my work" becomes "Having self-respect and high standards for whom I choose to work with."

"To work on myself and find a great partner" becomes "Sharing my love for personal growth with someone I love and respect."

As we'll see soon, these values work like light switches. When you run new ideas through them, they are either compatible or incompatible with those ideas. In other words, you will always know what to do.

If you don't spell out your own beliefs and values, you will always struggle to make consistently good decisions, and even worse, you will always second-guess your choices.

To understand why, let's pretend that you are a real estate broker, but you also love to travel and would like to become a travel blogger. If you value immediate business growth and being part of the local community, you can focus on your current business, and travel can wait. But if you value location freedom and adventure more than anything else, you can go all-in with your blogging and put your real estate career on hold.

Both options are perfectly valid, as long as you focus on only one. But if you don't prioritize, you'll find yourself dabbling with both and getting nowhere.

If you want to grow your business and enjoy your life, you need to take bold actions and stick to them in the long run. There's no room for second-guessing and retreats.

It's equally important to note that your value-priority scale can, and should, change over time. For example, if you are in the start-up phase of your business, you may temporarily prioritize working long hours at the office over lots of family time and vacations.

But when your business takes off and can run on its own, you may readjust your values to prioritize family time and leisure activities.

The important lesson here is to be mindful of what you want at a particular stage of your life and have enough integrity to stick to the values that support that vision.

Trust me, once you get good at labeling your values, you will know when it's time to sit down and reevaluate them. Think about the last time you had to go somewhere, but you really didn't want to. You probably counted down the minutes until you could leave, and although you were physically there, your mind was in a completely different place.

That's how you feel when you act against your values. So, as long as you pay attention to your thoughts and emotions, you will always know when it's time to adjust your priorities.

Create Goals That Align with Your Vision

Now let's look at how to set great goals worth working toward. See, in my years of coaching and running my business, I have realized that the vast majority of people who don't accomplish their goals are not lazy. On the contrary, if they work with a coach, they are probably action takers! So why are they still failing to get results?

There are two essential items you need to address before

setting a goal:

1. Does your goal align with your vision?

2. Is this the right time to aim for this particular goal, or are there other goals that need to be taken care of first?

For now, let's look at the first point. Say that your vision is to own a big chain of yoga studios with locations in all the major cities to help busy professionals fight stress and regain balance.

You've been working hard at launching your first location, then one day a friend tells you about a business opportunity in the restaurant industry. You and she analyze the numbers, and they make financial sense.

Would you go for it? We will cover decision-making in more detail in chapter 5, but for the sake of this scenario, the answer is "no."

I'm not saying that you should discard every opportunity that presents itself, but be mindful that most will not align with your vision. It's up to you to recognize which opportunities do align and to go for those.

In short, by making sure that any new goal you set aligns with your vision, you'll travel the shortest path from point A (where you are now) to point B (where you want to be.)

Figure 2 gives you a visual representation of goals that align with your vision and those that don't.

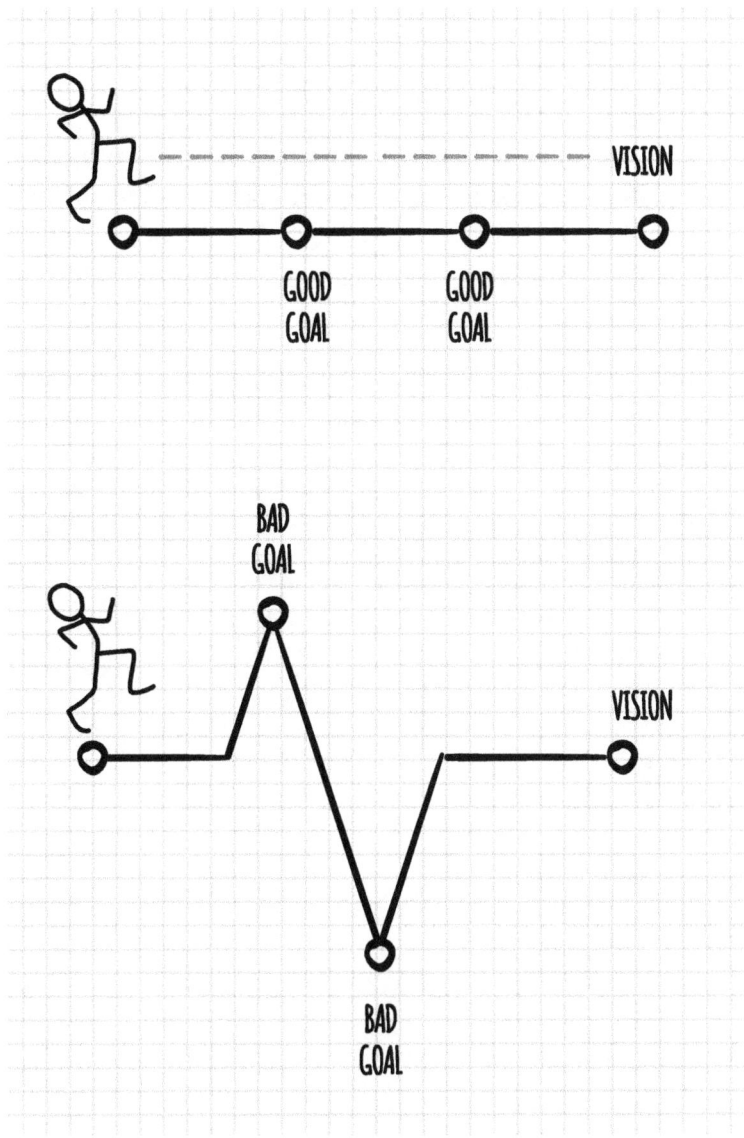

Figure 2: Goals that Align with Your Vision

Now let's look at the second item.

When you are working toward your vision, there will be some goals that align perfectly with it, but that doesn't mean that you can go after all of them at any time.

To show you what I mean, let's pretend that you are building a house. You will need foundations, wall framing, a roof, plumbing and electrical work, insulation, drywall, flooring, windows and doors, a bathroom and kitchen, light fixtures, wall paint, furniture, and decor.

But even though these things are all necessary to complete your house, you wouldn't set the delivery date of your bedroom furniture on the day you start the excavation.

In other words, you need to follow a logical step-by-step process that allows you to build upon each goal.

Figure 3 shows the problem with failing to prioritize good goals.

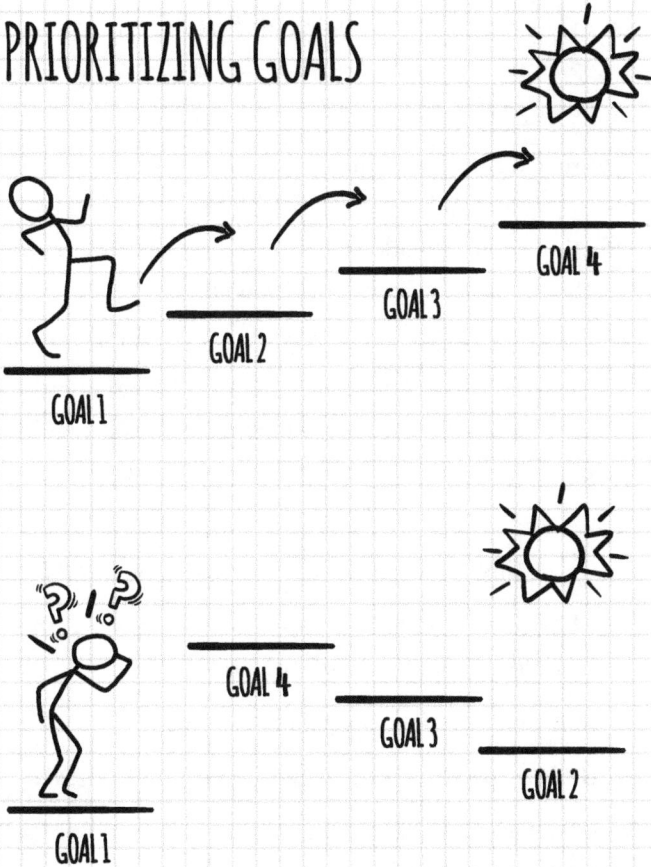

Figure 3: The Problem with Failing to Prioritize Good Goals

Too many entrepreneurs launch expensive ad campaigns before fine-tuning their brand messaging and building their reputation. It's easy to get carried away by the more exciting goals and to leave the rest to chance, but in doing so, you are greatly diminishing your ability to achieve lasting success.

You may experience some wins in the short run, but as soon as you step away to get a bird's-eye view of your overall progress, you'll see that you haven't moved much.

Now that we have explored the downside of not prioritizing your goals, let's look at how you can achieve success faster by carefully selecting what to work on first. To illustrate this, let me tell you the story of how I'm writing this book.

I had wanted to write a book for a long time, but I was always too busy. In 2016, I tried to write one during my recovery, but I was overwhelmed by the amount of writing it required, so I stopped.

Then, after I scaled my business, I suddenly had more time to focus on writing. But this time, I also had a much better plan.

First, I listed all the goals I needed to accomplish to finish the book fast, and this is what I came up with:

1. Find and articulate a problem to solve
2. Build a coaching framework to teach my audience
3. Come up with supporting stories to illustrate my points
4. Gather social proof and case studies to build trust and authenticity
5. Learn how to type fast to speed up the writing process
6. Get coaching on how to structure, launch, and promote the book

7. Find an editor and a publisher

8. Write 55,000 words in 30 days

Then I took a bird's-eye view of all these goals, and I ordered them so each could build upon the previous point and speed up the process. Here's how I organized them:

1. Find and articulate a problem to solve

2. Build a framework to teach my audience

3. Get coaching on how to structure, launch, and promote the book

4. Learn how to type fast to speed up the writing process

5. Come up with supporting stories to illustrate my points

6. Gather social proof and case studies to build trust and authenticity

7. Write 55,000 words in 30 days

8. Find an editor and a publisher

As you can see, I didn't even start writing the book until I had sorted out the majority of the supporting goals. And now that all the steps are in place, I have been writing at the rate of about 1,800 words per day, which means I should complete the entire manuscript in only 29 days.

The lesson here is to break your goals down into smaller action items. And once you do that, arrange them so they build upon each other, and the results will compound. This then leads to you being able to prioritize your work throughout the day.

Prioritize Your Work Based on Your Vision

If you are like most people, you live most of your waking hours on autopilot. From when you turn off the alarm in the morning to when you get back into bed, you repeat countless habits, some of which have been holding you back.

This book is not about forming good habits and dropping the bad ones, but it's essential to understand that the only way to live out your purpose is to execute small daily actions that align with your vision and goals. Writer and speaker James Clear explained this beautifully when he said, "Every action you take is a vote for the person you want to be."[3]

And since, when you repeat an action over and over again, it turns into a habit, we can say that your aim should be to carefully choose your habits and let the rest run its course.

The great thing is that you don't need to spend hours a day on each task to see results. For some tasks, as we're about to see, it could take as little as five minutes a day.

In fact, the key to sticking to your goals is to incorporate three types of tasks into your day:

1. Movers

2. Optimizers

3. Routines

A mover is an action that moves you toward your vision and your goals. For example, let's say that you want to scale your

---

[3] APB Speakers, "Atomic Habits: How to Get 1% Better Every Day—James Clear," August 7, 2018, YouTube video, 8:03, https://www.youtube.com/watch?v=U_nzqnXWvSo.

marketing agency to multiple seven figures. In that case, your movers will be things like cold-calling 50 businesses a day, hiring and training your sales team and your marketers, creating content, and appearing on podcasts to increase brand recognition. Prioritizing movers in your schedule is key to ensuring that you stay on the rise.

An optimizer is any task that allows you to optimize your life or workflow. For example, when I decided to write this book, I knew that I needed to step up my typing game. So after a quick Google search for the best site to learn how to type, I set aside 15 minutes after dinner to do my exercises for just 30 days.

After only one month, I had gotten used to typing the proper way. This temporary small change to my daily schedule is bound to save me countless hours in the long run.

This is going to require you to use some chess-like thinking. That's why you need to set aside time to think about what to optimize and plan how to do it. But when you get into the habit of doing this, the quality and quantity of your work will skyrocket.

And last, your routines are crucial to keep you grounded and in control of your days. We'll cover more about this topic in chapter 15, but keep in mind that when you turn your movers, optimizers, and routines into habits, you can be sure that results will come your way faster than you ever thought possible.

Now let's look at how one of my clients used this system to get himself unstuck and build the lifestyle of his dreams. When Liam and I started working together, he felt trapped in a stressful office job. Still, he knew that he wanted to be his own boss by launching a marketing agency, traveling the world, and eventually following his passion for the performing arts.

After assessing his situation, he decided that his best bet was to find a remote job and get back about two hours a day in commuting time.

Once he was working from home, he scheduled out his movers, optimizers, and routines. Then, every day before he started work, he planned his day, did some cardio, and meditated. When he finished his full-time job, he reached out to 20 prospects and took care of client work.

Within six months, he could already have quit his employee job, but he wasn't done yet. His goal was to travel while working, so he kept optimizing his schedule to get him closer to that reality.

He first set aside a daily slot to work on getting social proof so he could charge more and finally hire staff. Then he set aside a daily slot to master automation software. And once his business started picking up speed, he and his partner made time each day to research and compare work destinations. In less than a year, Liam was able to scale his agency, and since then, he has worked from dozens of locations all across Europe, the U.S., Mexico, and Canada.

As of 2022, he's been living in Vancouver, where he gets to hike every day and spend time in nature, and he's finally getting back into the entertainment industry.

Talk about living out your vision!

CHAPTER 4

PRIME YOUR SUBCONSCIOUS

Throw Out the Garbage

Now that you know how to build your vision and set the right goals, it's time to work on your subconscious mind. We briefly covered the subconscious mind in chapter 3 where you learned that this part of the mind doesn't know the difference between reality and fantasy.

That is why horror movies and haunted houses at amusement parks exist! On a conscious level, people are perfectly aware that the danger is not real, yet their subconscious mind thinks and acts as if it is.

To keep your mindset in check, you need to limit your exposure as much as possible to the news, social media, and negative people.

Of course, you can—and should—keep up with the world and financial news, but be mindful of what type of articles you consume.

The same thing goes for social media and negative people.

Whether it's constant complaining or pictures of unrealistic body types, these are all inputs that your subconscious ends up absorbing.

A 2020 study conducted by researchers at the California Institute of Behavioral Neurosciences and Psychology, Fairfield, states that "a number of studies have been conducted on the impacts of social media, and it has been indicated that the prolonged use of social media platforms such as Facebook may be related to negative signs and symptoms of depression, anxiety, and stress. [...] Furthermore, social media can create a lot of pressure to create the stereotype that others want to see and also being as popular as others."[4]

Let me show you how this can become a big problem if you don't address it.

Let's pretend that your goal is to scale a jewelry e-commerce business from two to 10 products and hit your first $100,000 month. To do that, you decide to work on this project nine hours a day for the next three months. Then, to recharge your batteries, you set aside two hours every evening for lots of self-care and quality time with your loved ones.

As time goes by, you are happy to see that you are showing up every day and that you are doing the work. But outside of your working hours, you are not taking care of your mind and body. Instead, you've been mindlessly scrolling through social media and spending hours watching 24/7 news channels.

You think about that for a second but then quickly tell yourself, "Oh well. It's not a big deal. As long as I'm working the right

---

[4] Fazida Karim et al., "Social Media Use and Its Connection to Mental Health: A Systematic Review," *Cureus* 12, no. 6 (June 15, 2020): e8627, https://doi.org/10.7759/cureus.8627.

number of hours, I don't need to worry about what I'm doing with my downtime!"

But at the end of the three months, you look at your sales reports, and you realize that you haven't made that much progress at all. You launched the new products, but they're not performing as you had hoped. That's when you decide to take a closer look at every decision you took over the course of the last 90 days, and you realize something.

Your initial goal was to build upon your high-end brand, but for some reason, you have been sourcing cheaper-quality products. But why did you do that? Those 24/7 news channels have been playing on repeat stories about high tariffs and trade wars. So, instead of you doing proper research and using logic, your subconscious mind hijacked your analytical thinking, and you acted out of fear by cutting costs and sourcing the wrong products.

Then you realize that instead of using social media to network with influencers and other brands, you have been watching viral videos and motivational memes. Sure, you showed up to work every day, but instead of working with clarity of mind, you went through the motions and completely lost sight of your original goal.

As you can see, working on the right things and with the right purpose in mind is just as important as showing up. But when you don't take the time to get back to your center, you slowly lose your ability to stay objective, you start making poor decisions, and worst of all, you don't even realize it's happening.

So, to avoid that, let's optimize your environment to protect your mindset.

First, try to notice and write down every time you check

your email, social media accounts, news apps, and other sources of distraction or negativity (including interactions with negative people).

If you are like me, you'll be surprised to see how much time you spend soaking up negativity every day.

After just a couple of days of doing this exercise, you will be much more aware of the attention traps you fall into and therefore know what distractions you need to protect your time from.

If your problem is watching TV after you get home, disconnect it, and cancel your cable subscription. If you can't manage your social media consumption, then get rid of all the apps from your phone! If you find yourself speaking with friends or relatives who constantly complain, but you can't just cut them off, try to reduce those interactions to a minimum. If you get sucked into a social media (or news) vortex when working on your computer, then install a news-feed blocker and a site blocker.

You may think that it's a bit extreme, but you are not aiming at being average, right? If you wanted to live like everyone else, you wouldn't be building a lifestyle business.

Bathe in Gold Daily

Once you have followed the guidelines above, your environment should be negativity-proof. But there's a problem. Every time you quit a bad habit, you leave a vacuum in your schedule. After all, if you were watching TV or scrolling through social media for hours every day, what are you going to do now? To avoid relapsing, you need to plan ahead by making a list of new habits you can default to when your old conditioning kicks in.

Let me show you how I kicked my social media and TV

addiction to the curb:

1. Replacing the morning news with an audiobook or podcast about health or business.

2. Going from watching random YouTube videos to reading interesting nonfiction books.

3. Switching Instagram and Facebook binges with journaling or taking online courses.

These are just a few examples, so feel free to come up with your own list of substitutes. The important thing is that you plan ahead, because when you feel the urge to pick up your phone or turn on the TV, it's already too late to brainstorm a replacement. For example, I have a list of over 20 different positive activities on my phone, and every time I'm about to slip into my old habits, I pick something from that list and try to turn it into a new habit.

I want to stress that this is not supposed to take too much time. Some of the activities on my list are as simple as reading my goals aloud or taking a three-minute cold shower. In fact, most of my self-care routines came from my need to replace old habits like smoking, watching TV, and sleeping in.

I like to refer to this process as "bathing in gold," and that's because every time I do one of these actions, I feel happier, stronger, relaxed, confident, and energetic.

It's crucial that you perform these routines daily because your subconscious mind needs repetition to reprogram itself. Just make sure that you don't turn this positive act into a perverse form of procrastination. The last thing you want is to fall behind on your business and life goals because you listen to too many podcasts or read too much.

This takes me to a question that a lot of my coaching clients like to ask: "Should I constantly look for new material, or should I consume content more than once?" That's a great point, so let me tell you what I do and what has worked with all my clients.

At any given time, I listen to or read about four titles a day—whether that's books, podcasts, or courses.

I read most business books once. For example, this month, I read four books about management and marketing. Then if I am trying to master a new tool or learn a new skill, I will take a course and possibly watch a few lessons more than once to make sure I understand everything.

But when it comes to my mindset, I only have four or five audiobooks that I like to listen to on repeat. See, my goal with these books is not to learn them on a conscious level. If that were enough to create lasting change, everyone who read Robert Kiyosaki's *Rich Dad Poor Dad* would be a millionaire. But to shift your mindset for good, you need to tap into your subconscious by using the power of repetition.

Rehearse Your Future Life

Reshaping your mindset through repetition works exceptionally well even when you act like your future self. That may sound a little odd, so let me show you what I mean.

Let's pretend that your goal is to launch a group coaching program, but you have limited experience speaking in front of an audience. You may be highly knowledgeable on the topics you coach, but when you try to record your content or get on a sales call, you sound and look tense. That's because your subconscious mind is still stuck in your old paradigm. In other words, you still don't see yourself as a successful coach because you don't yet have extensive experience.

Your prospects can't point out the problem, but they can't justify spending money with you, so you find yourself stuck with no clients and little self-esteem.

But then, one day, you decide to get in front of a mirror. You stand tall, imagine an audience in front of you, and start speaking with pride and enthusiasm. The first day feels good, so you decide to try it again the day after. Before you know it, you sound and feel great! You can't wait to record new ads, host new webinars, and launch a new program. Now your prospects see you as an expert and can't wait to learn from you.

Rehearsing your future self is so powerful for two reasons. First, you get to practice your craft and smooth out your delivery, and second, you implant new images and memories in your subconscious about who you want to be. And since the subconscious mind doesn't know any better, it will keep expressing itself through this new version of you.

My clients and I have been practicing many versions of this exercise. But so far, we have gotten the best results by pairing up the rehearsal method with our medium- and long-term goals.

To explain this, let's go back to the group-coaching example above, but this time, let's assign a three-month goal and a three-year goal. As a medium-term goal, let's say that you want to onboard 15 clients and have weekly Zoom calls with them. And as a long-term goal, you want to host a big, in-person conference with at least 200 people.

In this exercise, you will first close your eyes and imagine yourself 90 days from today on a Zoom call with your 15 clients.

Then you open your eyes and start acting as if you were on the call with them. Once you are done with the first phase, close your eyes again, transport yourself mentally to your conference three years in the future, open your eyes, and start acting as if you were on stage.

This process can take as little as five minutes! The important thing is that you genuinely feel as if you were there. I am not talking on a physical level, of course, but on an emotional one. And since your subconscious is the primary driver of your thoughts and feelings, the more you practice, the easier it will be for you to step into the role and feel like the person who has achieved those goals.

I am not going to lie—when I started doing this, I felt ridiculous! I stood staring at myself in the mirror and didn't know what to say. But the more I practiced, the more I could come up with creative plots to act out.

Since I am writing this book, one of my medium-term goals is to launch it and promote it through podcasts, interviews, and video ads. So before going to bed, I go on my patio for five minutes and pretend that I am being interviewed. I go through every possible question I can think of, and answer with the same passion or excitement I'd have in real life. Then I switch to the video ad, and I act as if I am filming it by brainstorming and freestyling a basic script.

I hope you are starting to see how powerful this quick habit can be in reshaping how you see yourself and therefore achieving your goals faster. Figure 4 is a visual representation of the process.

MOST PEOPLE

BIG GOAL

SELF-IMAGE

YOU

TIME + WORK

BIG GOAL

SELF-IMAGE

YOU HAVE TO RAISE YOUR SELF-IMAGE TO THE LEVEL OF YOUR GOAL

TIME + WORK

YOU CAN'T OUT-PERFORM YOUR SELF-IMAGE

Figure 4: Rehearsing Your Future

Make Mindfulness Your Thermostat

Now that you have the tools to fix how you see yourself, let's look at how you can control your mood.

Your mood can often change throughout the day, and it does so very quickly. You could be having a great morning, but then at lunch you read something that throws you off, even just a little, and for the next couple of hours, you are on edge.

When the mood change is drastic (e.g., when you find out that someone you know died), you also experience an intense change in how your body feels (a strong emotion). But if the mood change is more subtle (e.g., a friend didn't reply to your message), your emotional reaction is not as strong, and you may not even realize that you are in a bad mood until much later.

When left unchecked, these mood swings can affect your life and business more than you think. After all, if you don't notice these changes, you can't curb them, and your mood will be at the mercy of your own environment.

So, if you want to nip your mood swings in the bud, you need to refine your ability to perceive your emotions, and the best way to do that is by practicing mindfulness.

Mindfulness is the ongoing awareness of your thoughts, feelings, and emotions—in other words, the state of being aware of what's going on in your mind and body at all times.

To prove to you why mindfulness is so valuable for managing your mood, let's first remember three facts:

1. Your thoughts and ideas come from the conscious mind.

2. Your feelings and emotions reside in the subconscious mind and the body.

3. Your mood is a long-form manifestation of an emotion.

The sequence goes like this. You first have a thought, or you get exposed to an outside stimulus. In turn, this perception or thought creates a physical manifestation that we call emotion. Once the new emotion sets in, your mood will change accordingly. But the mood can persist long after the emotion is gone.

And so, what happens if you practice mindfulness? You still have that thought or stimulus. That event still triggers a physical reaction and creates an emotion. But since you trained yourself to feel even the most subtle change in your body, you can shine your awareness on that process and break the tie between the emotion and the mood.

It's like when you discover how a magic trick works. You can still watch the show, but you are not emotionally invested in it. Let's pretend that you are in a meeting with your sales team, and one of your reps decides to quit in front of everyone and makes a scene. Your initial thought is "Who does he think he is?!" You start to breathe heavily, and your blood pressure rises. You're about to turn aggressive. Then all of a sudden, an alarm goes off in your head, and a little voice says, "Something is wrong. We are losing control!" In a split second, you realize that you were letting outside circumstances control you. You take a moment to clear your head, reframe the situation, and deal with the matter in a much more calm and effective way. After the incident, you walk away happier and more confident than before. That's the power of mindfulness.

You've probably heard of mindfulness if you've ever meditated or took a yoga class. That's because you can't meditate or have a good yoga session without being mindful. But you can easily be mindful without having to meditate or do yoga.

In fact, you can sustain a significant level of mindfulness throughout the day without having to set aside time to practice. And since there's no barrier to entry, you have no reason not to try. So let me show you how.

As you sit reading this book, all you need to do is bring your attention inside your body. Do you feel anything? If you are entirely new to this, you may not even know what to look for, so let me help you.

Can you feel the blood pumping in your hands, arms, or legs? What about your feet? Can you feel a slight tingling somewhere?

If you don't feel any of that yet, that's ok. It will take a couple of minutes to fine-tune your perception. But in the meantime, focus on your breathing instead. To do that, try isolating two things: first, the cold air flowing in through your nose and into your throat, and second, the air that pushes down into your lungs and expands your rib cage.

You can do this at any time throughout the day, for example, while you're driving, walking, or in conversation with someone. And the more you practice it, the easier it will become, and the more benefit you'll get from it.

Associate Yourself with Winners

The last step to priming your subconscious mind is to rewire yourself to seek "pursuit" as your baseline status.

Most people's baseline status is "rest," meaning that if you let the average person do whatever they want, you'll soon find them relaxing somewhere.

Case in point, I grew up like many other kids in the 1980s

with three TVs in the house. As soon as my father would get home from work, he'd do some chores around the house, and then he'd sit in front of the TV. Then we'd have dinner, we'd tidy up, and boom! Back on the couch to watch TV until bedtime. Growing up, I've always found myself defaulting to the living room.

When I decided to quit my job and start a side hustle, I struggled quite a bit with fighting this urge. After a day in the office, instead of working on my business, I'd grab a snack and chill.

Then after about six months of poor results, I decided to attend an entrepreneurship event in Toronto where I met two agency owners and became pretty close with them. We spoke at least once a week, and every conversation we had was charged with ideas, plans, and success stories. Whenever they talked about a big deal they closed or the new team member they hired, I felt guilty because I was not putting in the same effort. Within a month, I felt a strong urge to raise my standards, and although initially I went about it in the wrong way and overworked myself, those connections helped me get over my tendency to procrastinate, and then they stuck with me until I got my act together.

You've probably heard the saying that you are the average of the five people you hang out with the most, but if that's true, how can you maximize the time you spend with those who push you to the next level?

If you have some time and a budget for it, go to a live event! I haven't been to one in years because I've been in Europe since before the COVID-19 pandemic, but that's hands down the best way to rub shoulders with like-minded people and build lifelong relationships.

If you can't go to a live event any time soon, the next best thing is to join a Facebook group in your niche and provide value by asking and answering questions. Be consistent with it, continue the conversations on Messenger, and you'll soon have a great network.

The same thing goes if you are building your personal brand on YouTube or Instagram. Be active in your community, and you won't lack inspiring friends. But I must issue a warning here: social media is like fire. It can be an extremely useful tool, but you need to handle it with care. When you use it, stay present, and if you feel as if you are getting sucked into a leisure rabbit hole, set a timer, get the job done, and get out!

As we wrap up this chapter, let me tell you about my client, Lucas, who was struggling with scaling his marketing agency. His sales were low, and he was charging less than he was worth. He had some fantastic testimonials already, so we knew this was mainly a mindset issue.

As part of his action plan, he moved from his small town in Eastern Canada to a bigger city. He took a personal inventory of his relationships at home and at work and was very mindful of who he let in his life. During his spare time, he built confidence and self-worth through meditation and rehearsing the life he was after. Then he networked his way into a small group of local entrepreneurs that kept him accountable. All these steps compounded enabled him to have his first $25,000 month in just over six months.

In his best-selling book *Zero-Resistance Selling*, Dr. Maxwell Maltz explains this phenomenon incredibly well when he writes, "You cannot outperform your own self-image."[5] So if you want to improve your results, first fix your mindset.

---

[5] Maxwell Maltz, *Zero-Resistance Selling* (New York: Prentice Hall Press, 1998), 131.

CHAPTER 5

DECISION-MAKING

The Problem with Too Much Data

N ow that you've set your goals and primed your subconscious, it's time to learn how to make better decisions. We briefly covered decision-making when we discussed choosing the right goals, but that was just one application.

In fact, in a single day you make more decisions than you can count. From what outfit to wear, to driving vs. taking a cab, or choosing what to eat for dinner, if you can't make up your mind quickly, you waste time. In terms of how indecision affects your goals, it will slow down your business growth, and you could miss out on some great opportunities.

Some types of decisions require a lot of data. For example, in marketing, knowing how to interpret lots of data is the difference between being profitable and losing money. But with most decisions, having too much data is a problem.

If you always had a ton of data to make all your decisions and a way to quickly analyze it, that'd be great, but you don't. So when you find yourself with limited information, you wait to make a decision—and then you wait a bit more.

This is no big deal if we're talking about a trivial choice, but what if you had a time-sensitive business decision to make?

In real life, you are not only rewarded for the quality of your decisions, but also for the speed at which you take them.

Let's say that you are drafting a proposal for a big client, and you stall on a small detail because you can't find enough data to back it up. A couple of days go by, and you finally get all the information you wanted. You finish the document, and you send it over. But a few minutes later you get a reply that says, "Thanks, but we already went with someone else."

Like my mentor, Craig Ballantyne, says, "Success loves speed," and most times, waiting for all the data slows you down. So the next logical question to ask is "How much data is enough?" In over 10 years of analyzing my clients' performance, and my own, I have learned that there's a sweet spot, and that's about two-thirds of the total data you can get.

When we launch Amazon products, for example, we look for pockets of opportunity in the market. And since the data is available to all sellers, we must act fairly quickly to get ahead of the competition.

In fact, some of the brightest minds of our time use similar approaches.

Colin Powell's 40–70 rule says that you should make a decision when you have between 40 percent and 70 percent of the available data. Deciding with less than 40 percent is no better than guessing. But anything more than 70 percent is unnecessary.

And in the 2016 Amazon shareholder letter, Jeff Bezos wrote,

"Most decisions should probably be made with somewhere around 70 percent of the information you wish you had. If you wait for 90 percent, in most cases, you're probably being slow."[6]

Learn How to Use Your Values

Another crucial tool for making better decisions is your values. We saw how a good set of values can help you with goal-setting, but how can you use them to make faster and better decisions?

First, realize that you can have different sets of values for different applications. For example, you can have values for your work and a set of values for how to be a parent. So take a look at what area you struggle with the most at making decisions, and list out all the values that apply to that area.

Now that you have these lists, you can use them in the same way we discussed them in chapter 3. But this time let me show it to you with a more mundane decision. Let's say that a relative you haven't seen in a while calls to say she'll be in town on Monday and invites you to a pub at 9 p.m.

Now let's look at three sets of values that are relevant to the decision you make about seeing her.

- Work values: focus, consistency, being on time

- Personal values: sobriety, eating healthy, sleeping well

- Family values: love, support, connection

With this information, you can quickly come up with an

---

6   Amazon Staff, "2016 Letter to Amazon Shareholders," Company News, April 17, 2017, https://www.aboutamazon.com/news/company-news/2016-letter-to-shareholders.

answer that makes everyone happy. You can still meet Aunt Susie, but you can ask her to meet you a bit earlier for a coffee, or you can stop by right at 9 p.m. to say hi, drink tonic water, and leave. If your bedtime is set in stone at 9 p.m., and she can't meet you before that, then you can decline the invitation and try to reach out to her in the near future.

Or what if you need to hire a web developer, and you are down to two candidates? The first charges less, but they only communicate through a messaging app, whereas the other is more expensive, but they plan on doing a screen-share call twice a week to get feedback and show their progress. If your values are speed and good-quality relationships instead of cutting costs, at this stage in your business, the choice is obvious.

No matter what decision you make, if you arrive at it from a foundation of clear values, you won't feel bad about making it because none of the alternatives make more sense.

But, before you start making better decisions, there are three critical points to consider:

1. There's a big difference between making decisions confidently and loving every decision you make. More often than not, a decision involves compromise, so it's a matter of knowing what you're prepared to compromise on.

2. Your values will change over time, so don't be surprised if you don't end up making the same decisions twice. What you wanted for yourself when you were a college student may be different from what you want now.

3. Making decisions that don't align with your values doesn't feel right. So if you still find yourself second-guessing your decisions, you may have been using someone else's values and thought they were yours.

As you can see in figure 5, values are like valves that can either let an idea through or block it. You can line up many valves in the system, and each valve can be completely open (it fully aligns with the idea), completely closed (it totally clashes with the idea), or half-open (could align with the idea but needs a compromise).

IDEA 1
OPPORTUNITY TO WORK AWAY FROM HOME FOR 2 YEARS

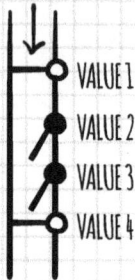

- VALUE 1
- VALUE 2
- VALUE 3
- VALUE 4

IDEA 2
TRAVELING WITH YOUR FAMILY WHILE RUNNING YOUR BUSINESS

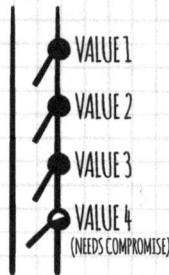

- VALUE 1
- VALUE 2
- VALUE 3
- VALUE 4 (NEEDS COMPROMISE)

IDEA 3
WORKING LOCALLY AND LIVE IN A BIG HOUSE

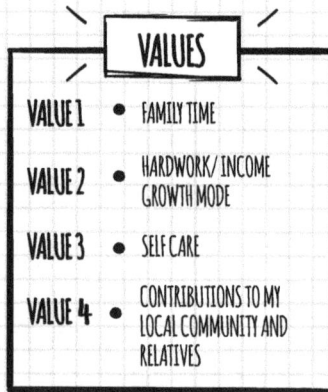

- VALUE 1
- VALUE 2
- VALUE 3
- VALUE 4

VALUES

VALUE 1	•	FAMILY TIME
VALUE 2	•	HARDWORK/ INCOME GROWTH MODE
VALUE 3	•	SELF CARE
VALUE 4	•	CONTRIBUTIONS TO MY LOCAL COMMUNITY AND RELATIVES

YOU CAN CHANGE THE PRIORITY LEVEL OF EACH VALUE OVER TIME I.E. IF YOU WANT TO BUILD YOUR WEALTH UNTIL YOU'RE 35 AND THEN FOCUS ON BUILDING A FAMILY, YOU CAN CHANGE THE PRIORITY OF THE RESPECTIVE VALUES.

Figure 5: Values

Avoid Shiny Object Syndrome

Having clear values and the right amount of data won't help you if you let your emotions enter into the mix. To avoid this happening, protect yourself with these three actions:

- Beware of shiny object syndrome (SOS)
- Recognize your bad days
- Practice resilience

As David Finkel describes it, *"shiny object syndrome is a condition that inflicts millions of business owners each year. Instead of focusing on the big-picture tasks that fuel growth for their business, they get sidetracked by a new business idea or project that feels new and exciting."*[7]

In chapter 3, we used the example of the yoga entrepreneur who got pitched by her friend about opening a restaurant. The numbers looked great, so that's the perfect example of a shiny object. But shiny objects don't need to be as big as opening a restaurant. They don't even need to be business related. What if your vision was to lose weight and start running marathons? Would you then sign up for a six-month baking class just because your friends are excited about it and want you to join?

Shiny object syndrome is so common because most of us are brought up believing that humans are born with a finite set of skills.

That means that the average person who embarks on a new

---

[7] David Finkel, "Entrepreneurs May Be Particularly Susceptible to Shiny Object Syndrome. Here's How to Cure It.," *Inc.*, January 16, 2020, https://www.inc.com/david-finkel/entrepreneurs-may-be-particularly-susceptible-to-shiny-object-syndrome-heres-how-to-cure-it.html.

project expects one of two outcomes. They'll either get good results because they are talented or get poor ones because they don't have an aptitude for whatever they're trying to do.

So, instead of maintaining a positive attitude and practicing with the intent of getting better, they get frustrated and start looking for the next opportunity in the hope that it will be easier. The cycle continues indefinitely, and that's why the average person spends their life working on dozens of small projects without ever bringing one to fruition.

An *Entrepreneur* magazine article from 2017 warns readers of the symptoms that you need to watch out for if you think you have SOS.[8]

- Inability to finish projects
- Poorly planning your ideas and directives
- Burning through cash
- Confusing your staff

To combat this unproductive pattern, when you are making important decisions in life and in business, avoid getting caught up in SOS by asking yourself two questions:

- Should I move on, or should I finish what I started?
- Is this alternative truly better, or is it just new?

If you often find yourself having to make the same type of decisions (e.g., which diet to start, what kind of business to launch, what sport to play), you may be affected by SOS, and that's okay.

[8] "Do You Have 'Shiny Object' Syndrome? What It Is and How to Beat It," *Entrepreneur*, February 9, 2017, https://www.entrepreneur.com/article/288370.

Now admit it, and do something about it. I had SOS for many years! In 2006 alone, I tried to become a magician and then a tango dancer, and then I took Japanese language lessons, and I have absolutely nothing to show for any of it.

I am not saying that you need to stick blindly to one project. If you don't see any results and are sure that you have given it your all, it only makes sense to move on. But at least the decision will be backed by logic. It won't be dictated by your emotions.

Acknowledge Your Bad Days

The other bias that you need to watch out for when making a decision is your own mood.

I don't have to tell you how radically different you could feel from one day to another. You may have been on a winning streak for a few weeks, and you feel unstoppable, then you hit a couple of roadblocks, and even the perception of losing momentum puts you on the defensive. Suddenly every bold decision that used to feel easy now feels like a gamble.

Plus, even things like the amount of sleep you had, temperature, humidity, and light can influence your mood. Since there are so many variables, you need to learn how to make sound decisions no matter what your frame of mind.

There's a reason why the top performers in any industry are disciplined both at work and home.

To avoid getting caught up in your emotions, ask yourself three questions:

1. "Has anything compromised my mood or attitude today?" This is the discovery phase, so be honest because

it's only about you.

2. If you realize that something is bothering you, figure out if it may interfere with your decision, and ask yourself, "Should I wait to make this decision until I am no longer emotionally involved?"

3. If the answer is "yes," but you can't afford to wait much longer, then try to change your point of view by asking, "How would I see this matter if I were in a confident and abundant mindset?"

In 2015, I closed down a fashion affiliate blog that I had worked on for almost a year. Sales were coming in, and I could have easily turned it into a $5,000 per month passive income stream, but I got caught up in a dispute over my affiliate pay. After I lost sleep over it for a couple of days, on the third morning, I closed the site and stopped posting. I reasoned that it was taking up too much of my time when, in retrospect, I was just having a bad couple of days.

Mood swings are real, and they will take control of your reasoning if you let them. But you can do a few things to either minimize bad days or minimize making decisions when you don't feel like yourself.

As a general rule, try to sleep well and eat nutritious food. If you live in a place where you don't get much sunlight, take a vitamin D_3 supplement and try using a light-therapy box to enhance your mood. We'll cover diet and sleep in chapter 16, but for now, keep in mind that these are fundamental in controlling your mood.

But whether your mood is stable or not, avoid making important decisions when you are hungry. In fact, in a study led by

Dr. Benjamin Vincent of the University of Dundee, researchers found that "hunger significantly altered people's decision-making, making them impatient and more likely to settle for a small reward that arrives sooner than a larger one promised at a later date."[9]

In other words, when your basic needs are not being met, you'll seek disproportionally higher amounts of instant gratification in other areas that you do have control over.

Practice Resilience

And this takes me to my last point: you need to practice resilience. The *Oxford English Dictionary* defines resilience as "the capacity to recover quickly from difficulties,"[10] which is essential on so many levels. But especially with decision-making, you can't let your past experiences dictate how you see your future.

As an entrepreneur (and a human being), you are bound to encounter setbacks, so the key is to learn how to bounce back quickly and maintain a positive mindset. As a beautiful quote often attributed to Winston Churchill goes, "Success consists of going from failure to failure without losing enthusiasm."[11] The key to that quote is the word "enthusiasm" because, without it, your decisions will lack conviction, and you'll act with a scarcity mindset.

---

[9] "Don't Make Major Decisions on an Empty Stomach, Research Suggests," University of Dundee, September 16, 2019, https://www.dundee.ac.uk/stories/dont-make-major-decisions-empty-stomach-research-suggests.

[10] Lexico, s.v. "Resilience," accessed June 13, 2022, https://www.lexico.com/en/definition/resilience.

[11] David Guy Powers, *How to Say a Few Words* (New York: Doubleday, 1953), 109.

So if resilience is the key to guarding your thinking against setbacks, how do you get good at it?

The process that we teach our coaching clients is very similar to mindfulness. As you know, when you practice being mindful, you bring your attention to the body, and you keep it there as you go about your day. So when internal conditions change (e.g., levels of stress, anxiety, or sadness), your awareness "thermostat" lets you know that you are getting off balance. There are three important behaviors that help you stay on track with being mindful:

1. Non-judgment

2. Re-centering

3. Gratitude

Non-judgment is the ability to not label feelings, situations, or people. Let's pretend that you're about to treat yourself to your favorite taco salad. You get it every Friday, and you are so excited! But when you finally make it to the restaurant, you find out it is closed. Your first reaction is probably sadness, and you may even get annoyed. But if you practice non-judgment, you realize that attaching any label to the situation is both useless and counter-productive. In fact, the act of judging takes you away from what is within your control: doing something about it or accepting it and moving on.

The next step is to get back to center, no matter how many times you get off course. Your goal is not to avoid being derailed; instead, accept that it will happen at some point and know you will get back on track, just as a pilot realigns the plane every time the wind knocks it off course. So when you identify negative thought patterns and compulsive thinking, replace them with focused awareness.

The final behavior is gratitude. Practicing gratitude, even once a day, at night or in the morning, will prime your mind with abundance and possibility, and those feelings will last the entire day.

When you adopt them consistently, these tools will make you virtually unshakable to outside circumstances. Of course, this doesn't mean that you will turn into a soulless robot, but you'll be able to gain strength from any challenge that comes your way.

SECTION 2
BRAND RECOGNITION

CHAPTER 6

CREATING CONTENT

Start with Your "Why"

Most of the clients who come to us are struggling for three reasons:

- They need more sales.
- They're not able to charge more for their services.
- They are working around the clock.

Of course, every situation is different, but more often than not, there is always one root cause: brand recognition. Having a solid brand is why Starbucks can sell their coffees at almost 40 percent more than their competitors.[12]

In his best-selling book *Start with Why*, Simon Sinek points out that "if you look back at the history of Starbucks, it thrived not because of its coffee but because of the experience it offered to

---

[12] Graham Rapier, "Starbucks Gets Away with Expensive Coffee in the Morning—but It's Losing Out to Cheaper Competition in the Afternoons (SBUX)," Yahoo! Finance, June 27, 2018, https://finance.yahoo.com/news/starbucks-gets-away-expensive-coffee-203600805.html.

customers. [...] Schultz had been enamored of the espresso bars of Italy, and it was his vision of building a comfortable environment between work and home, the 'third space,' as he called it, that allowed Starbucks to single-handedly create a coffee-shop culture in the United States that had until then only existed on college campuses."[13]

Starbucks charges more because of the problem it solves and the name it has built for itself, not because it uses a rare quality of coffee beans. People will go to great lengths to associate with a brand they know, love, and trust. So if you are experiencing any of the above issues, build a brand around a big "why" that your audience can believe in, and everything else will be much easier to handle.

Now let me show you how that works. Let's say that you are a CPA offering simple bookkeeping, payroll, and tax returns. You are tired of charging just enough to pay your bills, and because you can't afford any help, you are working 15-hour days. The issue is that there's a sea of other accountants who can replace you at any time. After all, what's the difference between you and them? So, to stay afloat, you compete on price.

But what if instead of following the herd, you raised yourself above it? What if you became the go-to expert in your market by helping your prospects solve a big problem (e.g., helping dentists build generational wealth with their practices)? You can create content for your market that relates to their struggles and shows them that you have the know-how and tools to help them. Now your prospects see you as a separate offering from your competition, so you can command higher prices, which leads to bigger profit

[13] Simon Sinek, *Start with Why: How Great Leaders Inspire Everyone to Take Action* (New York: Penguin Group, 2009), 221.

margins, which lets you hire a team and free up your schedule.

If you're ready to elevate your brand presence, let's look at the first step: creating content.

Creating good content is the most reliable and stable way to build your brand. But the secret to making it work is first to figure out who your audience is and why they should care. If you are a doctor, for example, don't just create general health content. Instead, pick a problem you want to solve and build a community around that topic.

When I first started the podcast, it was called *Up Your Game*, and we covered everything to do with productivity and business. We had some success, but as soon as we focused on helping solopreneurs build lifestyle businesses, we resonated with a specific audience and got a lot more exposure.

If you run a local business, your community is already defined geographically, so you can immediately tailor your content to your audience. Bradley did exactly that with his show, *Toronto's #1 Real Estate Podcast*. He started creating hypertargeted content to help people in the Greater Toronto Area navigate the local real estate market. Within months he had grown his brand, started closing more deals, and monetized the show. We'll dive deeper into his story soon, but for now, let me address a common concern.

One of the questions I often get is "Why would someone come back to me if I give away all my knowledge?" And the answer is that people like to know the solution to a problem, but they will willingly pay for someone else to solve it or guide them through the process.

If you are a lawyer, for example, and you are making videos about employment law, your followers will learn a lot from them, but if they need help, they'd still need to hire a lawyer.

And it's not only like that for professional services. During the COVID-19 wave in 2020, Zoom fitness classes and webcam personal training services skyrocketed. But why is that? You can find all sorts of workouts for free on YouTube! It's because people like to pay for convenience.

Know Where Your Market Hangs Out

Now that you have found the "why" for the content you are creating, it's time to look for your perfect client. I know that between Google and Facebook Ads, targeting has become more of a science than an art, but you don't need to overcomplicate things with software just yet.

Let's pretend that you launched a new golf apparel line and wanted to promote it in person. What would be the first logical step? You'd probably make a list of golf courses and start from there. After all, those are the places where your perfect clients hang out.

Doing this online is no different from doing it in person. The advantage of the internet, however, is that you can be in countless hang-out spots simultaneously. From forums and Facebook groups to Instagram hashtags and YouTube comments, you won't run out of ideas if you know how to look.

But what if you don't get the results you want right away? Don't be discouraged. Let's bring everything together to make your content explode. For optimum impact, you need to align these three elements:

1. Your audience

2. Your message

3. Your medium

What if you are a dietitian helping overweight dads lose weight and keep up with their kids? Your audience is defined, and your message is spot on. But you are making long YouTube videos that busy dads don't have time to watch, so you're still not getting much traction.

The point I'm making is that, in the beginning, you want to test as many combinations of these three elements as possible. We'll talk about automating your content creation later in this chapter, but for now, keep in mind that you should try at least a couple of different combinations of your audience, your message, and your medium.

Pro tip—try to keep up with new format releases on the social media platforms you use. For example, Instagram released Reels in August 2020, and YouTube followed in March 2021 with YouTube Shorts.[14] Both formats were created as a response to and to keep up with the rise of TikTok. As a content creator, it makes sense that you test powerful new channels you have at your disposal, but this doesn't mean that your target market will automatically resonate with them, so be aware of new trends and test with an open mind.

The best way to test your content is to cover a couple of different topics, create a few versions of the posts (e.g., short- and

---

[14] "Introducing Instagram Reels," Instagram, August 5, 2020, https://about. instagram.com/blog/announcements/introducing-instagram-reels-an-nouncement; Todd Spangler, "YouTube Shorts at One Year: What the Video Giant Has Learned About the 60-Second Format—and What's Next," *Variety*, October 15, 2021, https://variety.com/2021/digital/news/ youtube-shorts-one-year-monetization-creator-fund-1235090053/.

long-form videos, images), and then distribute them across the platforms you want to test.

Let's say you are a solar contractor, and you want to educate people on the benefits of switching to renewable forms of energy. First, you'd create and test two topics: how to operate the systems and how to get the proper permits. Then for each topic you'd test different platforms, hashtags, and keywords to dial in your audience, and you'd also test the format with your videos, images, and audio.

In the beginning, this will take some time, but stay with me because it will get much easier and faster once you hit the right combination. Once you reach this point, you'll be able to automate your content by working on it for less than two hours a week.

Consume Other People's Content

And this takes us to another roadblock for many of my clients: Lack of ideas!

I remember when I told a good friend that I would create daily content. He looked at me and said, "How on earth are you going to come up with hundreds of things to talk about?" But at that point, I had already been following several content creators and reading dozens of books in my niche, so it was only a matter of organizing my thoughts and writing them down.

But you don't have to read a book a week like me to be prolific. All you need is a quick and easy content consumption strategy.

First off, choose a platform you like (I use Instagram) and follow only hyper-relevant pages in your niche. I recommend using a business account so you don't mix up your personal and business networks. Depending on how large your market is, you should come up with a follow list of between 20 and 40 accounts.

Now go through your news feed every couple days, and save the posts that most align with your message. This is not supposed to be a long session. You are going in to get ideas, not get an education. Remember that you are already the expert.

If you are a veterinarian, you don't need to sit through a 10-minute video about how to deal with fleas. I hope you already know how! But the "How to Deal with Fleas" title should help you brainstorm a couple of good pieces of content—for example, "What to Do if Your Cat Has Fleas," or "10 Things to Avoid When Your Dog Gets Fleas."

But titles are not the only thing you should focus on. If you are on a platform that shows you how popular a post is, then get ideas from the topics and keywords that did best. Depending on what platform you are searching, things to watch out for are views, comments, likes, and shares.

But now that you have lots of ideas for content, you may be wondering, "Why would people listen to me if there are so many other content creators out there?" There are two reasons why.

1. You have carved a clear subniche, so your knowledge gets applied to a specific circumstance.

2. Different people resonate with different content creators. You'll attract those who resonate with you.

If everyone were afraid of copying others, we'd only have one business for each niche. Would you not open a burger joint just because there was another one in town? Sure, having two McDonald's side by side may be redundant, but how many times do you see a Burger King close to a McDonald's? People like options. So as long as you have a viable market, and you're adding your personal touch, your content will attract the right audience.

Become Omnipresent

By now you should have an idea of what platforms and what post formats to use. The next step is becoming omnipresent by automating and delegating the majority of the work. If you are a one-person show, don't worry! You can still get most of this system on autopilot with little effort on your part.

First, set aside either an hour a week or a half-day every month to batch your content. Batching is the process of coming up with days or weeks of content in one sitting. There are two benefits to this process: you don't have to carve out daily slots for content creation, and also you'll have a bird's-eye view of your upcoming material, which will give you a more balanced profile. Once your content is created, you can schedule the posts to go live at a later time. Most platforms have their own content-management tools, but if you want to control everything from one software, you can use a tool like Buffer or Hootsuite.

Once the posts go live, though, you want to invest some time engaging with your audience and niche. The last thing you want is to do all this work and then miss out on the opportunities you created!

Batching your content may seem like an overwhelming task, but if you break it down into bite-size actions, you'll be done in no time.

My mentor, Craig Ballantyne, first showed me this method, and since then I have perfected it to fit my posting needs. First, you come up with the five key ideas you want to post about, and then you find six ways to convey them.

To show you what I mean, let's use my coaching business (The Remote CEO Academy) as an example. Here are my five key ideas:

1. Brand recognition

2. Remote team-building

3. Sales and marketing

4. Mindset and decision-making

5. Lifestyle design

And these are the six ways to convey the ideas:

1. A testimonial

2. A personal story

3. A quote

4. A lesson

5. A pep talk

6. A case study

Now, all you have to do is combine each key idea with a way to convey it, and voilà! You just made your thirty posts for the month.

If you have access to a team, then you can use the text-first or video-first approach to repurposing your material. As you can see in image 8a, the text-first method lets you create one blog post that can be turned into infographics and used as a script for a long-form video. Then you can take snippets from the video and turn them into Reels or Stories. You can also take the audio and turn that into a podcast episode.

And if you prefer being on video more than writing a blog post, you can use the video-first method in figure 6. Here you first record a five-minute video, use it for short-form and audio content, and then get it transcribed and turned into a blog post and an infographic.

CONTENT STRATEGIES

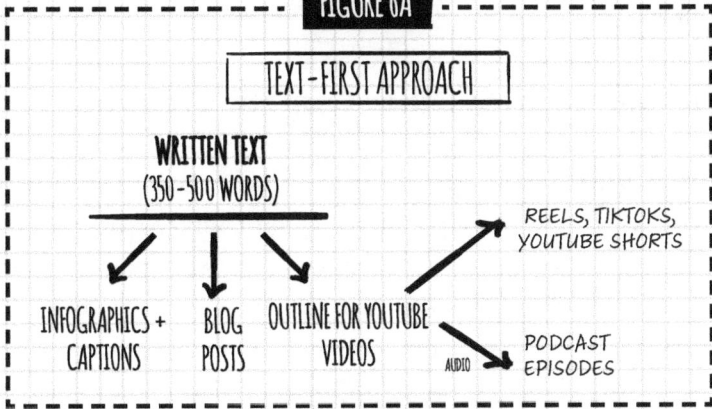

FIGURE 6A

TEXT-FIRST APPROACH

WRITTEN TEXT
(350-500 WORDS)

INFOGRAPHICS + CAPTIONS

BLOG POSTS

OUTLINE FOR YOUTUBE VIDEOS

REELS, TIKTOKS, YOUTUBE SHORTS

AUDIO → PODCAST EPISODES

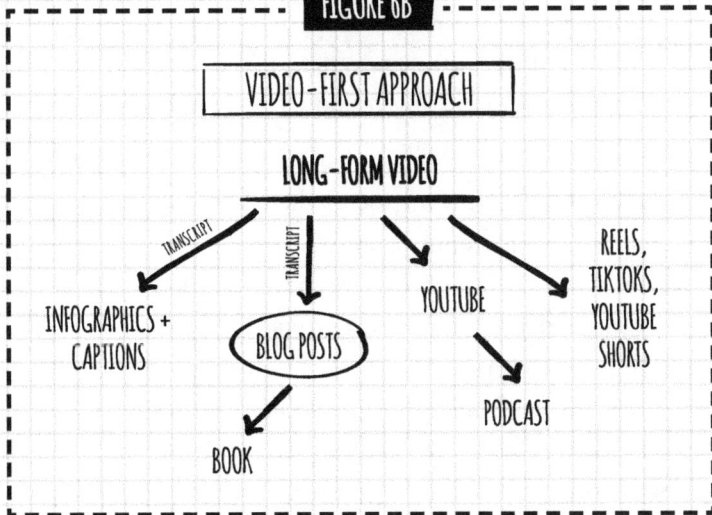

FIGURE 6B

VIDEO-FIRST APPROACH

LONG-FORM VIDEO

TRANSCRIPT → INFOGRAPHICS + CAPTIONS

TRANSCRIPT → BLOG POSTS → BOOK

YOUTUBE → PODCAST

REELS, TIKTOKS, YOUTUBE SHORTS

Figure 6: Video-First Method

As a rule of thumb, quality is more important than quantity, so if you don't have any help, focus on two platforms first. Then, once you hire an assistant, you can train them on how to edit your content to fit other media, leaving you free to branch out.

Partner Up with Other Content Creators

At this point, you're ready to create your content calendar, but there's one more thing you need: a community. Earlier in the chapter, I warned you about posting and not engaging with your followers, but that's just the beginning. If you want to grow an engaged community, you have to network with other public figures.

While you can network on all platforms, podcasting is hands down the best way to interact with other creators. Podcasts are perfect for interviews and medium-length conversations. So as long as you stick to producing good-quality content for a few months, you can start hosting your own interviews and eventually go on other podcasts as a guest.

If you want to dip your toe in the water, you can get a decent-quality USB microphone on Amazon for under $50 and sign up for a platform like Libsyn or Podbean to upload your content to be distributed across all the major podcasting platforms. Once you have your podcast cover, intro, and description, you can record a few solo episodes to set the scene. And when you have a couple of months' worth of content, you can sign up for a site like Podmatch or Matchmaker to network with other creators and start booking your interviews.

Let's pretend that you are a psychologist. After three months of posting solo episodes, you decide to invite other experts to your podcast to discuss mental health issues. Every time you interview someone, they share the episode with their network. A few months after that, your podcast is getting noticed, and you finally get to interview big authors in your field. Could you think of a more effective way to rub shoulders with the giants in your industry?

The benefits of working with other creators go beyond the increase in the size of your audience. In fact, there are two more consequences that beat vanity metrics: authority and mentorship.

The authority that you develop in your market is one of the most critical assets in your business. It lets you charge higher prices and allows you to close more deals. For example, as a junior lawyer, you may be onboarding one client at $1,500 every eight sales calls, but now that you have built your name, your conversion rate can get to one sale every four calls, and you may charge $3,000. That's the difference between losing money on ads and becoming extremely profitable.

The other advantage is mentorship from the people you interview. Think about the value of talking to your guests before the show and learning about their experiences, and then carefully choosing your interview questions. That habit will make for a great-quality podcast, but it will also allow you to get incredible insights right from the source.

Since you already know how crucial my own podcast was to growing my brand and business, let me give you another example.

Earlier in the chapter, I briefly mentioned Bradley and his success with *Toronto's #1 Real Estate Podcast*. Now I want to show you how his simple process made him an authority in his market.

Bradley made solo YouTube and Facebook videos about real estate for quite a long time. He had been getting some traction, but he wanted to take his reach and impact to the next level, and

SMART BUSINESS, BETTER YOU

that's when he decided to go all-in with a podcast. For his interview episodes, he invited investors and real estate developers, and for his solo shows, he analyzed news articles about the Toronto and Canada markets.

Within three months, he had a lineup of guests who couldn't wait to be on his show. But that was just the tip of the iceberg. Bradley was about to become the middleman between his guests and his listeners who wanted in on the deals—what a great position to be in!

CHAPTER 7

WRITING A BOOK

The Fastest Way to Influence Your Niche

Another way to build a lasting brand and influence your niche is to write a book. This can seem like a daunting task, but the truth is that if you already possess the knowledge, you are not far from being done. If you create a solid layout with clear topics to cover, the chapters, and the subsections within the chapters, all you need to do is write 1,000 words a day, and you can finish it in just over a month. Yes! You read that right. A 2014 article on The Nonfiction Author Association's website explains that the average word count for a traditionally published nonfiction book runs between 50,000 to 75,000 words, while self-published nonfiction books can be as small as 20,000 words.[15]

And if you are not sure that small books can make an impact, think of the *Art of War* by Sun Tzu, which is just shy of 10,000 words, or *The Four Agreements* by Don Miguel Ruiz that caps at

---

[15] Stephanie Chandler, "How Long Should Your Nonfiction Manuscript Be?" Nonfiction Authors Association, April 7, 2014, https://nonfictionauthorsassociation.com/how-long-should-your-nonfiction-manuscript-be/.

less than 35,000 words.

Trust me: if you have something worth sharing, your audience won't care if your book is 170 pages or 300.

So, you made up your mind to write a book, and you're ready to create your outline, but you have one more question: "How do I structure my topics?"

Don't forget that as a solopreneur scaling your business, you are writing a book either to win clients or get speaking gigs. That means that your manuscript will cover the topics that you're already dealing with on a day-to-day basis.

Let's say you are a physiotherapist who helps people with back injuries to walk again. And because you want to grow your personal brand and influence more people, you decide to write a book. The good news is that you already go through a few routine treatment stages with your patients, which might look something like this:

1. Tell the patient why this treatment is more effective than others.
2. Build trust by talking about your experience.
3. Start with upper-body exercises and describe the benefits.
4. Share inspiring stories of people who fully recovered.
5. Continue with lower-body exercises.
6. Assign more exercises to do at home.

We are now getting very close to the basic outline of the book. You have a problem that you can solve, your background story, several exercises that you can split into a handful of chapters, and a final chapter to summarize everything. Then sprinkle all this with social proof to show that your system actually works.

To complete the outline, go inside each chapter and write 10 to 15 bullet points you want to talk about, and congrats! You are ready to write your book.

The Easiest Ways to Write a Book

But what if you are not ready to write an entire book yet? Maybe you're still developing your frameworks, or you're too busy to put your thoughts down on paper. Can you get started any other way? Sure you can! Here are three nonconventional ways to get your first book out fast.

Collecting Blog Posts

If you've been writing a blog for more than a year, congrats! You should already have more than 50,000 words covering a wide variety of subjects in your business. All you need to do is pick the most successful blog posts and spend some time linking them together. Then write an intro chapter and a conclusion, and you are done. Mark Cuban's first business book, *How to Win at the Sport of Business*, is, in fact, a collection of his best blog posts.[16] Sure, he may have more street cred than you, but it's how the stories are linked together that makes the book flow exceptionally well.

Collecting Interviews and Transcribing Them

This is the technique that I used when I wrote *10 Millionaire Mentors* (more about this later). If you have a podcast or a YouTube

---

[16] Mark Cuban, *How to Win at the Sport of Business: If I Can Do It, You Can Do It* (New York: Diversion Books, 2011).

channel where you interview people, you have a ton of great content that your guests share with your audience. So why not turn that into a book? Start with relistening to your favorite episodes and time-stamping the sections you want to feature in the book. Then use software or hire someone to transcribe those sections.

The trick here is to pick interview answers that cover different topics. For example, if you are writing a book about dog training, look for answers that cover principles of dog training, training puppies, training adult dogs, dominance-based vs. relationship-based training, etc. You can then organize the chapters by topic or expert you interviewed.

Dictating Your Book and Getting It Transcribed

If you don't want to type your book, you can record yourself talking about each chapter in detail. For this method, make sure that the text is adapted to a written style when it gets transcribed. To make the process easier, use the outline you already have and expand on each bullet point a bit more, so you don't have to take too many pauses to think about what to say.

This is a great method, especially if your book doesn't have too much technical information, because you can be done in just a couple of days if you are crystal clear on what the book is going to be about.

Another fantastic side effect of dictating your book is that the text will be naturally engaging. In fact, one of the biggest problems with new writers is that their material sounds too impersonal.

The Publishing Path

Once the first draft is complete, you will have to face the age-old question: to self-publish or not to self-publish?

But if you are writing a book to grow your business, the self-publish route is the best one for many reasons.

First, when you self-publish, you control when the book is released. That seems like an obvious perk, but when you work with a publisher, they can decide to delay the launch for months or even years! Can you imagine working hard to finish your manuscript on time and finding out that it won't be out for two years?

Second, if you thought that going with a publisher meant that you didn't have to do the marketing yourself, you'd be wrong. Unless you are a professional author with a large audience, you are still responsible for promoting your book online and off-line.

And third, self-publishing allows you to keep the majority of the profits for yourself, which means you'll have more money to reinvest in ads, promotions, and other marketing costs.

This is not to say that publishers aren't a valid option. If you are writing a book for mass consumption, you are not on a specific schedule, and you already have a large community, then getting a publisher to do all the work for you makes sense.

Get Instant Credibility

But regardless of how you publish, having a book gains you instant credibility. That's because most of your competitors are still just dabbling in social media and maybe podcasting.

Don't get me wrong, I love creating content for my social

platforms, but you can't deny that having a business account on social media has a very low barrier to entry, making it hard to stand out. But when you couple your social media presence with a book, that's when heads start turning.

This takes me to the biggest hurdle in a solopreneur's journey to writing a book: impostor syndrome. In fact, the most common objection I hear is "Why would someone read my book?" And my reply to that is always the same: "You are not writing a book for your entire niche. Your target market is people who know less than you about the topic."

Let's pretend that you are a midwife writing a guide to help women through pregnancy and delivery. You collect your personal experiences and hard knowledge in a book and market it to … pregnant women. See? You didn't write it for medical professionals. In fact, your audience wouldn't want to read a technical textbook about pregnancy. It'd be way too elaborate for their information needs.

The best way to keep that in mind during the writing process is to pretend that you're speaking to a client. Did you notice that this entire time I have been writing to *you*? You are the person who needs guidance. So it makes sense to keep things personal and mimic a one-on-one conversation with a client.

But now that you've finished your book, what's next? As a thought leader in your industry, you can leverage it to get speaking gigs, new clients, or to sell more products. Let's look at all three options, and keep in mind that the more creative you are, the more opportunities you'll spot.

In 2020, I wanted to get speaking gigs and onboard more coaching clients. I was starting my coaching career at that time, and I wanted to run a few tests to get proof of concept. So I put together a collection of the 10 best interviews from my podcast, and I called it *10 Millionaire Mentors*. Instead of printing this book, I sold it as an audiobook and e-book combo for $15 through a sales funnel. That was enough to keep the ads running and get new coaching leads. Then I reached out to business incubators and offered my material for free, and within weeks I was also getting speaking gigs. Keep in mind that this wasn't even a full book! We had just collected and transcribed existing material. As we saw earlier, you can get very creative with how you write your book.

Speaking of funnels, Russell Brunson (the cofounder of ClickFunnels) started releasing a series of books shortly after launching his company in 2014. The books teach entrepreneurs how to master online marketing and sales funnels and have sold hundreds of thousands of copies. But that's not it! The readers loved his books so much that most of them ended up using ClickFunnels, and now the company has over 100,000 paying users.

Multiply Your Chances of Getting Interviewed

Can a book increase your credibility regardless of how many you sell? The answer is "yes!"

Podcasting is now mainstream, and hosts always look for a good guest. And since the market is becoming crowded, podcasters are getting pickier with who they interview. In fact, when we sift through applicants at *The Remote CEO Show*, we always prioritize two types of people: those who run a big lifestyle business and those who wrote a book about a topic that we like to cover.

And these interviews aren't only going out on podcast platforms. They get listed on Google and other search engines along with the show notes. So as long as you secure a few appearances, you'll get great search engine optimization for your name, and that will increase your credibility.

But podcasts are not the only way to get exposure for your book. Opportunities are everywhere. From blogs and YouTube channels to magazines and industry websites, you are just a few clicks away from booking your next interview. We'll cover how to get press in the next chapter, but for now, let's focus on the best practices for getting interviewed.

As a rule of thumb, keep your messaging consistent across your interviews. You should have your key points on repeat so that your new audience knows exactly what to expect from your book. You also want to use stories to support the points you are making, but make sure that they are quick! And last, find out how long the interview will be and keep that in mind when answering your questions to ensure you fit in what you want to say.

I've interviewed hundreds of guests since I started my show, and although I'm grateful for all of them, I've had my fair share of awkward moments. But instead of revealing all my stories, I'll give you a list of things to avoid when being interviewed.

- Don't share too many details about your personal life unless they directly relate to the book.

- Don't give extremely short answers. Even if the hosts ask you a yes or no question, elaborate on it by tying it back to one of your book's messages.

- Don't give overly long answers. If you talk about your entire book in one answer, the host won't know what follow-up questions to ask.

- Don't show up to the interview with lousy audio quality.

Invest in a good mic (and a good internet connection).

- Don't give an interview without first researching the show. Find out if they need you to be on video and research their audience.

That's it! Now you can share your message with the world like a pro.

The Economics of Your Book

Once you get your book edited and published, you have a great new tool in your marketing arsenal, but what are you going to do with it? Always keep in mind why you wrote the book in the first place. Unless you are a professional author, you shouldn't see the book as your primary source of income. Sure, it's going to be a great new income stream, but the goal of your book is to generate leads and increase credibility and status. And to make that happen, you could even give away some copies of books for free.

Let's do the math and see why it may make sense. In the past 24 months, our average cost per lead using LinkedIn Outreach and YouTube Ads has been around $10. And since these leads just met me on those platforms, they had limited knowledge of my coaching program.

But since you can order hardcover books in bulk at $15 per unit, you can give away 10 of your books as a networking tool and generate at least three leads from them. Plus, these leads can then read your book and have a much better idea of what you do.

But if you don't know who to give the books to, you can use the free-plus-shipping model and upsell the buyer with the audiobook version. We used a similar version of this offer in 2019 and

SMART BUSINESS, BETTER YOU

were able to pay for our lead-generation ads for over nine months. This is also the method that Russell Brunson uses to get his books into the hands of over 100,000 people.

You first target your audience with an ad about the free book. Then you send the visitor to a page that explains what the book is about and clarifies that the only thing you pay for is the shipping. Once visitors add the book to their cart, they get the option to also purchase the audio version for $15. And so, even if one in seven people buys the audio file, you'll make enough money to keep running the ads, which get you more leads.

But what if you want more referrals? A book can help you with that as well. When we were selling the audiobook of *10 Millionaire Mentors*, I gave away a free copy to each of my clients, and I also told them to gift it to their entrepreneur friends. That same month we had a significant spike in podcast subscribers and inquiries about our coaching program. This is just from an audiobook! But the effect is amplified when you give away physical books. Depending on where your clients live, you can gift them the books in person or send them via mail. Just tell them to keep a copy for themselves and give one to a friend.

We now covered the many ways to write a book and just as many techniques to sell it or get business from it. You have no excuse not to get started! If you are committed to growing your brand, you'll have to write one sooner or later. So why not start now?

CHAPTER 8

GETTING FEATURED

People Do Research Before Buying Anything

In 2012 I was working in sales for a start-up, and one of my good friends left the company to work in corporate sales. After a couple of months, we bumped into each other, and I asked him how things were going at the new job. The first thing he said was "Not good. They gave us a script to convince prospects not to look at our reviews online. We have quite a few bad ones, and we've been losing lots of sales because of it."

First impressions matter, and in a world where everything gets rated and looked up, you must take care of your reputation on Google. In the 2020s it's not enough to untag yourself from party pictures and embarrassing videos. You have to proactively build and maintain your presence as an expert in your field. So, if everyone searches you or your company, they're going to be assured that they are doing the right thing by working with you.

But 2012 was 10 years ago, and only part of the population knew how to look up companies online. Fast forward to today, and even 80-year-old grandmas are reading and leaving reviews of their favorite stores. It just makes sense to Google a company before investing time and money on it. It takes two seconds, and it could save you from making a big mistake. But this is good news for you. In fact, you can develop an exceptional search engine–results page for your business and then encourage your prospects to Google you.

Kim took these lessons to heart when she started running her physiotherapy business remotely. She spent a few months working on her online presence and securing written, audio, and video interviews to discuss the problems she helps her clients solve. And as a result, within three months her consultations went from stressful sales calls to frictionless onboarding calls.

But even when people get good press, they often share it with their personal network once, and then they forget about it. What a waste of a great sales tool! Why not share your articles on your social media accounts every once in a while? I promise it won't look like you are bragging if you do it the right way. It's a great way to get engagement. All you need to do is preface the link to the article with a message that addresses the topic you covered and how you can help. Then, put a question to your audience. This way you create context for the article, and the post looks more natural.

And if you do outreach on a platform like LinkedIn or Instagram, make sure you share your press often so when people click on your profile, they can clearly see all your features and appearances.

Don't Hire a Public Relations Firm

You're starting to see how using public relations (PR) the right way can help you win clients. But how do you get PR anyway?

And do you need to hire an agency? The short answer is no. But that's because, eventually, you will want to have a team member working on that area.

When you hire a PR agency, you are outsourcing two things: the know-how and the connections in the industry. When an agency takes you on as a client, it starts pitching your story to its network of media writers. Agencies also need to keep in touch with their network and make sure to stay relevant. Of course, all of this takes time and expertise, but most agencies charge $10,000 a month on average. And if you are scaling your business, I can think of plenty of better ways you could spend that money. So before you decide to work with one of them, you should try putting together your own system for getting press—once your team learns the basics and builds a network, they can get the job done for a fraction of the cost.

But let's remember something before we dive into the process: media writers are content creators, and as such, they're on a schedule to come up with new content every day. That means that if you position yourself as a reliable source of information, they'll be the ones looking for *you*.

With this in mind, your goal is to make a list of industry magazines and publications, then follow their social media accounts and bookmark their sites. Now go through their articles and find out who wrote them. These are the people you want to network with and provide value to. Start with reaching out through Twitter or email. Stay genuinely interested in them, and when you've built some rapport, let them know that as an expert in that niche you'd love to help them with some of their work.

When you get your chance, the key is to act as quickly and efficiently as possible. Reporters often work on multiple articles simultaneously, so they like to work with readily available experts.

Earlier, you read that Kim was able to get lots of press in a matter of months. But I didn't tell you that she also secured TV appearances and national press coverage. And she did all of it on her own with the systems we taught her.

"At the beginning, I had to do some extra work to find out what media outlets fit my brand and message. But once I had worked on the network, everything else clicked, and I started to get noticed," she said.

So, before diving in headfirst, remember why you are doing all this. It's supposed to help you get better clients and close more deals, but it's only one piece of the puzzle. The last thing you want is getting caught in a PR rabbit hole for months and using it as a way to procrastinate on your sales and lead generation.

The Art of Getting Featured

Now that you know how to get publicity, let's see how you can build your network.

The first step is to be crystal clear on how you want the world to see your business. Once you have that in mind, you need to look for at least five angles to build your opportunities around. Think of your business as an island that has no way to communicate with the media across the sea. The only way to change that is to create bridges to link your business to the press. Each bridge is a story you tell to make your business relevant to a specific topic. The more stories (or angles), the more topics you get to chime in on.

Let me show you what I mean, but before I do, take a look at figure 7.

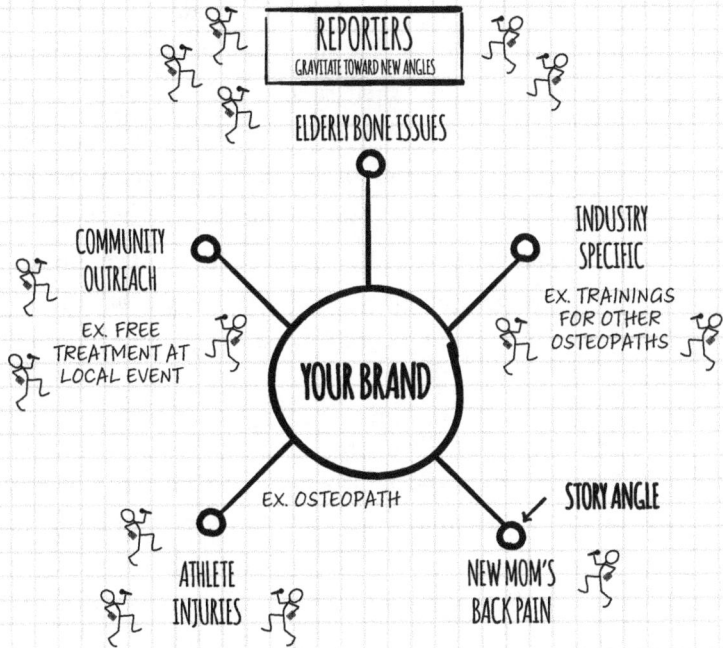

REPORTERS
GRAVITATE TOWARD NEW ANGLES

ELDERLY BONE ISSUES

COMMUNITY OUTREACH
EX. FREE TREATMENT AT LOCAL EVENT

INDUSTRY SPECIFIC
EX. TRAININGS FOR OTHER OSTEOPATHS

YOUR BRAND

EX. OSTEOPATH

STORY ANGLE

ATHLETE INJURIES

NEW MOM'S BACK PAIN

THE MORE ANGLES YOU CAN FIND FOR YOUR BUSINESS,
THE MORE CHANCES YOU GET TO BECOME A RELEVANT SOURCE.

USE THESE ANGLES TO BUILD YOUR NETWORK.

Figure 7

As you can see, an osteopath can get publicity from many angles. For example, she can appear in a sports magazine, a local newspaper, an industry-specific platform, a maternity website, and more.

Now you see why this system takes some time to set up. But like all good investments, it will generate dividends for years to come. Once you have your angles, start researching media outlets in those niches and follow their social media accounts. There are two main ways to keep up to date with their releases. One is Twitter, which is a massive hub for journalists and reporters. You first want to follow the media outlet itself, then, once you start learning the names of the reporters, you can follow them directly. The second way is to set up an RSS feed. They are a bit outdated, but there are no better competitors for staying in the loop with the latest articles.

Now that you know your targets, it's time to reach out. Keep in mind that reporters are extremely busy, so keep messages short and packed with value. You could start with some genuine praise for a specific article they wrote. Then relate it to how it affected your life or work. If you can help them in any way, do it. Keep it short, and don't expect an answer. After a few weeks, get back in their inbox with another helpful note. Once you get a reply, keep the conversation going, and let them know that you'd love to offer your knowledge and experience. And once you get your first article, make it a point to mention it to the other reporters when you are offering to help. You can write something like "Hey, _____, I'm sure I can help you with this. I already talked about this topic two months ago with _____ at *Forbes*."

Once you start getting coverage, it's time to let the machine run on its own. The testing phase should be over within a couple of months. Now you have two or three connections for each angle, and those are the only reporters you should catch up with every few weeks. If you provide real value, the reporters will come back to you. Some of them will even give you private insight on the stories they're working on.

It's About Credibility, Not Exposure

You now have enough connections to get as much press as you want. But one question remains: Can PR alone generate sales? The answer depends on what type of article we're talking about. There are different tiers of magazines and different types of articles. The best is a full-feature article about you and your business. Then there are mentions, which are articles that talk about a specific topic and cite you as the expert. In this case, you get to briefly share your knowledge.

So if you get a full feature in *Entrepreneur* magazine, which has a circulation of over half a million, then you could potentially build your brand overnight. But if you get simple mentions in a few local magazines and blogs, those may not be enough to generate an inflow of leads.

PR is a form of brand recognition—it's one of those things that you don't think you need until you don't have it anymore. But if you want to stay relevant, you must keep on hammering that nail. For example, Coca-Cola is one of the biggest brands in the world, yet, according to a 2021 study presented on Statista, "Coca-Cola Company spent 816 million U.S. dollars on advertising in the United States in 2019."[17]

Brand awareness is what amplifies your messaging. Think of

---

[17] "Coca-Cola Company: Ad Spend in the U.S. 2019," Statista, July 2020, https://www.statista.com/statistics/463084/coca-cola-ad-spend-usa/.

brand awareness as the size of your stage and the quality of your message. Once you build good brand recognition, every product you launch will come from a trusted and respected source. People will know what to expect when they buy from you, and this added layer of security makes every transaction easier.

Since sales don't come directly from your PR and brand recognition campaigns, it's easier to overlook this step and go straight to your paid ads to drive traffic to your offer. And that's why new businesses bleed ad spend and rarely become profitable.

As your features and mentions start to build up, it will be tempting to appear in as many articles as possible. In fact, it's great if you and your team can gamify the process—the only thing you need to be careful of is going off-brand.

In 2016, when I was introducing a few new kitchenware items to my online store, I decided to get some press for our brand. Within a couple of weeks, I had already gotten quite a bit of publicity. The problem was that instead of getting my brand name featured, I had made the mistake of using my name. So when I launched my ad agency a few months later, people searched for me online and could mainly see my kitchenware business instead of my agency. It took me quite a few emails, but eventually I got them to swap my name with my kitchenware brand.

Keep that in mind, and don't work on anything that can confuse your audience.

Balance Promotion and Creation

As I said earlier, your goal is to get a team member to do the PR work for you. So how should you structure the job for them? We're about to get into a whole section of the book that talks about attracting, hiring, and managing remote talent, so I won't go into the technical side of it here. But there are a few things to keep in mind.

Once you have a virtual assistant, you can train them on how to check your inbox and go inside the private groups to look for potential requests daily. This process should take just a few minutes, and it can be done as part of their end-of-day routine. Then, using a customer relationship management program or another productivity tool, they can send follow-up messages to the reporters in your network. Remember that reporters are busy, so this should be a quick message every month.

But don't forget that once your assistant finds a story for you to work on, you are the expert in charge of answering the reporter's questions. Some queries may be quick, but some articles may require hours of your time to answer correctly. Guard your time wisely!

Often my clients ask me if there's such a thing as too much exposure, and the answer is "no." The only indication you may be getting too much PR is if you're neglecting other important parts of your business. In that case, you either need to get your priorities straight or find a way to automate your PR process further.

And this takes me to my final point in this chapter: repurpose, repurpose, repurpose! You know how much time you can save if you reuse some of your content, so why not apply the same system to getting PR? You can do this by storing all your written content in a program where you and your team can access articles by topic or keyword.

I write all my blogs and emails (and even this book) with Penzu, a cloud-based journaling tool that my team and I can access from anywhere. Aside from some personal pages that I keep password protected, my team can easily search all my blogs and social media posts. So when a reporter asks me to comment on a specific topic, my assistant can pull up information from my old posts and tweak it a bit to turn it into a new answer.

Of course, make sure that the assistant who helps you get PR speaks and writes well. The last thing you want is to lose credibility because of someone else's grammar mistakes. If you want to allocate a bigger budget to this task, you can also hire a ghostwriter whose sole responsibility is to write on your behalf. And once your system is up and running, you'll enjoy ongoing publicity on autopilot.

SECTION 3

SELL, SELL, SELL

CHAPTER 9

FINDING YOUR VOICE

Believe in Your Product

A re you ready to enter the arena? You've built the foundations by working on your mindset, and you've built your brand by sharing your experience and knowledge. Now it's time to open the floodgates and grow your sales.

No matter how great you are at selling, you won't see outstanding results unless you really believe in your offer. I used to suck at sales! I dreaded every call, and even when prospects were cooperating, I found it hard to take control of the conversation. That was until I started seeing my clients getting unbelievable results. I was running an e-commerce marketing agency, so since my clients were getting a ton of sales and were paying very little for ads, I felt as if it was my duty to get more business owners on board.

Let me show you what I mean. Would you be excited if I asked you to go door-to-door to 10 homes to sell a random gadget? Not likely. But what if I told you to go door-to-door, to the same 10 homes, to let the owners know that they'd won $1,000? You'd probably have a good time breaking the news to them.

That's the difference between selling something you don't care about and something you genuinely care about.

But believing in your product doesn't just mean that you like it. When you can't possibly understand why someone would turn down your offer, that's when you're ready to sell. Sales is a transfer of emotion, so if you lack passion for what you're selling, the prospect won't be "passionate" enough to buy it.

It takes time for prospects to believe in what you offer, so the first step toward that goal is to provide an extraordinary consumer experience. Make sure to overdeliver to the point that your clients can't help but tell their friends.

Our clients at Gold Rush—my digital marketing agency—were, on average, getting a six-time return on their ads, but that wasn't enough. We wanted our less tech-savvy clients to better understand the results. We started by sending them branded interactive reports so they could see their best-performing products and ads.

Then we changed our offer to a performance-based service, which meant our clients would only pay us a percentage of the sales we delivered, and that's when I had my breakthrough: "Why would anyone say no to this?"

When you believe in what you're selling, you won't even see pushback as a bad thing. Instead, you'll be able to see it for what it is: inertia. People don't like change, and therefore they resist it. But if you don't fully believe that you have a fantastic product, the pushback will feel real. You'll start thinking things like "They may not be a good fit," or "The timing may be wrong. Maybe next summer."

Best-selling author, real estate entrepreneur, and sales coach Grant Cardone writes in his book *Sell or Be Sold*, "Become so sold, so convinced, so committed to your company, product, and service that you believe it would be a terrible thing for the buyer to do business anywhere else with any other product."[18] This is the secret that differentiates small-business owners from those who build companies that stand the test of time.

Let me give you another example of how easy it is to sell when you stand behind your product. Let's pretend that you are a doctor, and a patient comes to you with a broken leg. You confirm that they have a fractured femur, and you tell them to wear a cast for eight weeks. The patient is upset because they wanted to go on vacation at the end of the month. Would you give in to your patient's pushback and say, "Okay, I guess you're right. Forget about the cast." No! You would keep calm and talk some sense into your patient.

Sales Is a Transfer of Emotion

Now that you are 100 percent sold on your offer, what's next? There are plenty of salespeople who believe in what they sell, but they're still not good salespeople. In fact, there are two other dimensions that you need to dial in. The first is your energy, and the second is affability—in other words, your ability to be pleasant.

Figure 8 is a graph to show you how they relate to each other and where different salespeople fall in the spectrum.

---

[18] Grant Cardone, *Sell or Be Sold: How to Get Your Way in Business and in Life* (Austin: Greenleaf Book Group Press, 2012), 51.

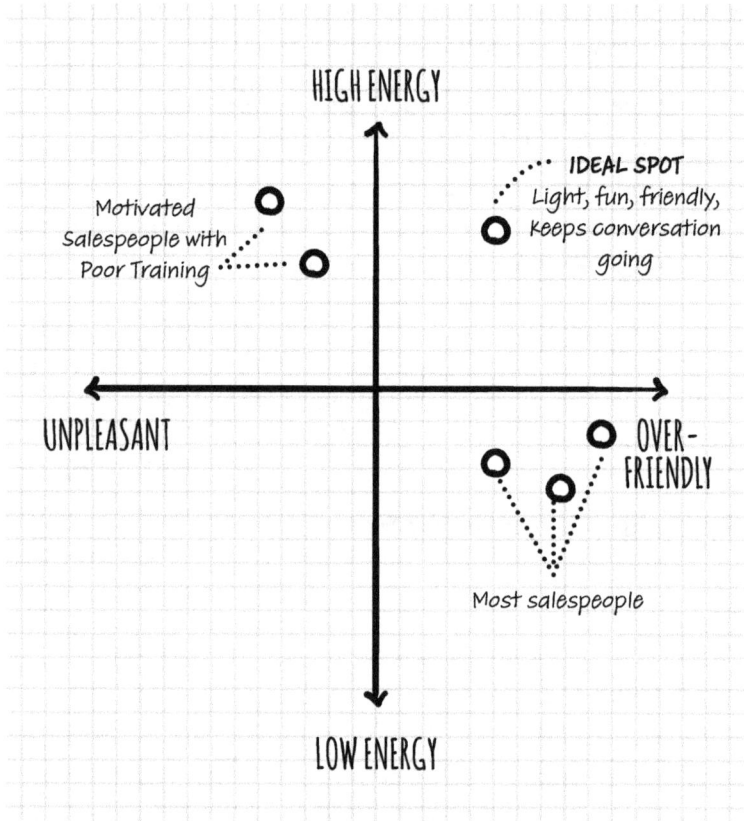

Figure 8: Dimensions of Salespeople

The *y* axis is energy. The higher up you go, the more energy you have. The *x* axis is affability. You go from being unpleasant, the far left, to being overfriendly, the far right.

The majority of new salespeople tend to fall in the lower-right corner, close to being overfriendly, to the point where they get pushed around. Sometimes they try to lead the conversation, but since they shy away from conflict, they tend to agree with the prospect the whole time until, inevitably, they lose the sale.

Some salespeople avoid the pushover stage, but they overcompensate for it by being too direct, and end up sounding desperate. Usually, this happens when the salesperson is under a lot of stress or is frustrated. Their energy shoots up, and they are focused on the sale, but if they haven't done adequate training, they run out of things to say and start repeating themselves. Ultimately, the prospect doesn't feel listened to, and the sale goes sour.

Then there's the ideal spot, which lies in the middle of the top right quadrant. You are energetic but not over the top, and friendly but in control of the conversation. You can build rapport, but you don't get lost in meaningless discussions. In other words, you are light and confident.

The key to getting to that spot and staying there is to have lots of things to say. We'll get to rehearsing soon, but for now, keep this in mind: the more closes and rebuttals you know, the longer you can keep the conversation going, and the more deals you close.

But how do you start a conversation on the right foot? The truth is that half of the work is out of your control. You don't know what the prospect really wants or what mood they're in. But you can control one thing: the questions you ask.

Rapport building is a powerful weapon, and like every weapon, it can end up hurting you if you misuse it. The easiest way to build rapport is by finding common ground with topics like cities you lived in, trips you took, your kids, and other subjects that come up naturally at the beginning of the conversation. Ask a question, make a remark, then move on quickly. But keep in mind that you may be able to use this information later in the call.

Another way to build rapport is by asking questions to discover why your prospect wants to buy. When the prospect answers, make sure to acknowledge them and possibly ask a follow-up question. This is a great way to show you are listening while getting more information.

When done right, by the time you are talking about your offer, you should know the exact reason why your prospect is there. That way, you can tailor the pitch to their situation.

Nobody Likes a Scripted Robot

A good sales call has many moving parts and variables, so how can you make sure you cover everything? Or even more importantly, how do you make sure your sales reps remember everything?

In most cases, the best way to standardize your sales process is by using a script. I know what you're thinking: "Scripts make you sound … scripted, right?" And you are correct. If you have ever received a call from a telemarketer churning out a long, convoluted script, you know that it can be pretty annoying.

But the benefits overpower the drawbacks. In fact, even if you are alone in selling your product, you need to monitor your performance, and you can't do that unless you keep every call consistent.

So, if you are serious about scaling, record your calls and test various versions of your script, at least until you master every section of the sales process.

While there's no one-size-fits-all script, a few elements are essential:

- The intro
- The discovery phase
- The pitch
- The clarification stage before pricing
- The price reveal
- Objection handling

The intro is where you set the tone for the call. Take this as an opportunity to take control of the conversation by asking the first questions and explaining what the prospect can expect.

The discovery phase is when you ask about their business goals and fears. Here you should find out what's not working for them and how badly they need that problem solved.

The pitch needs to be all about them. Sure, you are talking about your offer, but what's in it for them? Don't focus on the features—emphasize the benefits.

The clarification stage before pricing is where you answer their buying questions. Address every concern and don't move on until the prospects are 100 percent happy with your answers.

The price reveal is the turning point of the call. If you did everything right up to now, you might end up closing the deal right there. But most often, you'll have to keep going.

Objection handling is where 90 percent of deals close. Here you want to master lots of rebuttals and trial closes to make sure that you keep on going until the prospect is ready to become a buyer.

Now that you understand the importance of a script, let's look at how to prevent you from sounding like a robot.

There is, in fact, a way you can use a script while still sounding natural, and that's by dictating it. Simply open a tool like Google Docs, activate voice dictation, and speak your script into existence. Begin with the intro and work your way down to the objection-handling section.

Once you have dictated everything, go back and edit the draft to turn it into an actual script. Our clients get access to done-for-you sales scripts, but even if you want to make your own, this process shouldn't take too long.

The key is to practice often by reading your script aloud and tweaking it to fit your inflections. But since you dictated it to begin with, you should already sound natural.

Then every time you hire a new sales rep, give them your script, and invite them to go through the same process so they have their own version. Get them to practice it a few times with you, and show them how to edit the text to make it sound more like them. That way, your team will never sound like a pack of robots.

Rehearse with Others and By Yourself

Even with a script, I can't stress how important it is to practice. I met my wife when she had just started working in sales, and within six months she went from having zero experience to making six figures. She won multiple awards and was eventually recruited to train a global sales team. And when people ask Brianne what her secret is, she always says, "I just deliver the script with energy, and I don't get derailed. I know what I need to say next, I read it, I get ready for pushback, and I keep going."

There are no shortcuts. If you don't practice, your delivery will sound sloppy, and the prospect won't feel confident enough to buy.

The best way to practice is to schedule role-plays with your team or someone who can help you. But reading the script from the top every time will only help you polish the intro. The key to achieving excellence in your delivery is to isolate a section of the script and practice it until it sounds spotless.

That takes me back to my inside-sales days. Our sales director would walk into a big room and start every Wednesday meeting with the same question: "What is deliberate practice?" And each week, a rep would stand up and say something along the lines of "It's organized practice with the intent of getting better." See? We were not going through the motions. Instead, we'd look for every small mistake, identify areas for improvement, and iron out the delivery and the tone.

During those Wednesday meetings, management would play a call recording at random. If you were picked, you sat at the front, facing 150 people, and your coworkers had to pick your call apart.

It was so painful! But it was extremely effective. You don't need a big room full of people to get the same results, though. Just set aside 30 minutes every couple of days to relisten to your calls and find out what needs improvement. That's why call recording is such a critical tool. Every time you or your team finishes a call, play it back and figure out what mistakes you made and how you can avoid them next time.

Learn How to Deal with Objections

No matter how much you practice and how good you sound, you'll still get objections.

People will still tell you that they need to think about it, that it's a lot of money, that they didn't think they had to make a choice today, and more often than not, they will tell you that they need to speak to someone before making a decision, (even if this "someone" was never in the picture until you revealed the price).

That's just the prospect's way to defer their decision. But if they were genuinely not interested, they would just say something like "This is definitely not for me, thank you. Goodbye."

If you don't pick up on this hesitancy during your sales calls, you'll miss out on many opportunities because you believe your prospect has good reason not to buy.

Another reason people are reluctant to commit has to do with the fear of making a mistake. Some prospects fixate on the worst-case scenario, and even though they like your offer, they don't want to risk losing money. The best thing you can do for these people is to eliminate or significantly reduce the perceived risk of working with you.

If you can't offer them a 30-day money-back guarantee, you should spend some time coming up with other ways to make your prospect feel at ease. Even something like a short trial can be a powerful way to get your foot in the door.

In fact, in my first month running my one-on-one coaching business, I signed up 16 prospects for a two-week trial that consisted of one 30-minute call every week. At the end of the 14 days, 12 people signed up for the monthly packages.

Keep in mind that I didn't even have to go through a lengthy sales call with them. I essentially replaced the consultation call with my actual coaching services and tripled my close rate.

I totally understand if, up to this point, you have wanted to stay away from sales. Between the way Hollywood depicts it and the stories your friends tell you, selling looks like a thing that belongs to modern-day mercenaries. But it doesn't have to be that way. You have been pouring sweat and tears into creating your fantastic offer, and it deserves to be seen by more people. You deserve to be known for it. And it will be worth your while. It all starts with a few commitments.

Commit to reaching out to at least 20 people per day. Commit to engaging in at least three good conversations a day. And commit to running at least five sales calls a week. Once you hit these benchmarks, it's only a matter of time until you'll get enough sales to warrant hiring sales reps, and then scale from there.

And last, don't be fooled into thinking that you can outsource sales right off the bat. Sure, you could do that, but if you don't crack the code of selling your own product, why would someone else have any success at it? After all, you know it better than anyone else. First get to know your market, then develop your sales strategy, and only then hand it over to your team.

CHAPTER 10

THE AOS (ATTRACTION, OUTREACH, SALE) MODEL

The Secrets of Organic Outreach

Now that you are ready to speak to your market, let's see how to get a constant inflow of leads. Because of the rise in digital ads and funnels, you might consider cold-outreach systems, like cold calls, cold emails, and private messages over social media, as outdated ways to get leads. I believe it all boils down to two objections:

1. Why bug people with messages and emails? They can just click on our ads when they are ready to buy.

2. People already receive too many messages. They won't read mine.

First off, most people need a nudge to start considering a purchase, just as they need a nudge to buy after you reveal the price. So running ads and passively waiting for leads will not give you the best results.

Yes, it's true that paid ads can potentially reach millions of people a day. And it's also true that people's inboxes are more cluttered than ever. But so are their news feeds.

A study from 2015 cited in *Forbes* estimates that the average person is exposed to between 4,000 and 10,000 ads per day.[19] That is far beyond the number of personal messages we get daily, so if you want to get noticed, the odds are still in favor of cold outreach.

But that doesn't mean that you should start spamming entire directories. While it's evident that more conversations result in more deals, your time (and your team's time) is precious, and you should only spend it on opportunities that have potential.

To do that, invest some time in building your customer profiles and be hyperspecific with your questions—for example, what are their names? How old are they? Do they have kids? Are they single? What do they do in their free time? Do they listen to podcasts? If so, what podcasts do they listen to? Why would they need my product? What has prevented them from buying before?

Congrats! Now you know exactly who to look for, where to find them, how to speak directly to them, and how to deal with their objections. So pick your outreach platform, and let's go!

My favorite places for outreach are LinkedIn, Facebook, and Instagram because you can see people's profiles and prequalify them before sending out messages.

On LinkedIn, you can use Sales Navigator to create highly detailed lead searches in seconds. On Facebook, you can find

---

[19] Jon Simpson, "Finding Brand Success in The Digital World," *Forbes*, August 25, 2017, https://www.forbes.com/sites/forbesagencycouncil/2017/08/25/finding-brand-success-in-the-digital-world/.

prospects by joining groups in your niche, while on Instagram, you can find your leads through hashtags or by sifting through the comments section on niche-related accounts.

These outreach methods are most effective when you can build on the steps we covered in previous chapters and provide value at scale.

Your best bet is to create an e-book, free training, or a Facebook group that solves a particular problem. For example, if you are a doctor, you can put together some training and create an online community for women going through menopause. Then reach out to each person by sending a short intro message, and when they reply, ask them questions about their issue and let them know how you can help.

Once the conversation is on, you can send them your e-book, free training, or link to the community, and only at this point do you earn the right to ask for a call.

Become Attractive

Going through this process on social media is more practical than over email. In fact, on social media, people can see your face, your photos, and your network, so they'll be more likely to chat with you.

But not all profiles get treated the same. When I was in corporate sales, my LinkedIn profile was a glorified résumé. I just had my work experience and a couple of recommendations, and occasionally, I'd share a motivational quote. So, every time I connected with someone, I'd either hear crickets or get a very dry reply.

Then when I opened Gold Rush Social, I decided to step up my sales game, and I optimized my profile. I made sure that my profile picture and cover photo were on-brand. I used the head-lines and the About section on my page to tell my leads how I could help them, and most importantly, I posted often.

In fact, there's no substitute for showing up every day to serve your network. If you are looking to increase your credibility, start by creating content as we talked about in chapter 6. It's the rep-etition that brings people to associate you with the issue they are trying to solve.

Plus, when you have a lot of content on your profile, you can send it to your leads as teaching material. Let's pretend you are a CPA, and you wrote a post about the tax implications of running your business from abroad. If one of your leads tells you that they're thinking of moving to Mexico for a year, you can send them a link to your post to help them decide. And if you have been following my advice about building community, your posts should have plenty of likes and comments, which will make you more credible.

We're very close to getting you on the phone with your pros-pects. Your profile is optimized, you have been using content to build authority, and now it's time to make your offer irresistible. The way you do that is by posting a lot of social proof. I'm dedi-cating a section of this chapter to collecting and displaying your testimonials, but first, let's look at the benefits.

A few years ago, I had the pleasure to work with Protein Chefs, a meal-delivery company for the fitness industry. Their food was phenomenal, and their sales were good, but their acqui-sition cost was a bit too high. Then, the owners, Yuvika and Ron, tweaked one thing in their marketing strategy, and their sales exploded: they led their marketing with social proof.

See? They didn't run ads that said, "Our food is the best. Buy our food."

They had photos of real clients opening their boxes and saying things like "I can't get enough of Protein Chefs. I've been eating their meals for two months, and it's better than homemade."

Keep drumming up new videos or screenshots of conversations (ask first!), and don't just settle for a few. Every time a client posts about you or compliments you, share it on your platforms. Each video will speak to a different person, and you never know which testimonial will resonate with a prospect and get them on the phone with you.

Create an Outreach System

Now that your calendar is filling up with calls, it's time to scale your sales efforts and automate lead generation. And like any system, a lot of the steps need to be standardized, including the messages. But I want to be clear: standardizing conversations doesn't mean sounding impersonal. Let me show you what that looks like.

First, take a look at all the conversations you had, and try to find a pattern, both in how you ask questions and in how you answer your prospect's questions. Generally, the steps look something like this:

1. Introduce yourself with a message—prospect responds.

2. Share your quick background story, and ask about their background—prospect answers.

3. Acknowledge and ask if there's anything preventing them from achieving their goal— prospect answers.

4. Bring up your e-book as a solution to their problem, and ask for an email address—prospect answers.

5. Send e-book.

6. Follow up after two days and pitch a call.

Once you have your outline, create different versions of your messages based on the type of answers you get from your prospects. Let's pretend that you are a nutritionist, and you just asked someone what their 12-month goal is. If they reply that they want to lose 20 pounds, you could answer with a dull message like "That's great! I can help with that," or you could go with something like "What a great goal. My client Roman lost 25 pounds in nine months. I can show you how he did it."

But to write messages that are this relevant, you need to brainstorm all the possible directions your conversation can take. For our nutritionist, the answer categories would be weight loss, weight gain, gastrointestinal issues, etc. The finished product should be a list of conversation steps with different message versions for most of those steps.

Now it's time to plug this workflow into a tool that your team can use. For this system, my team and I like using Trello. The board view allows you to lay out lists from left to right. Each list represents a conversation step, and lists can contain cards. So when you create a card for each prospect, every time they answer, you can move the card with their name from left to right and keep track of hundreds of conversations at the same time. Image 3 shows how the system looks for those of you who haven't used Trello before.

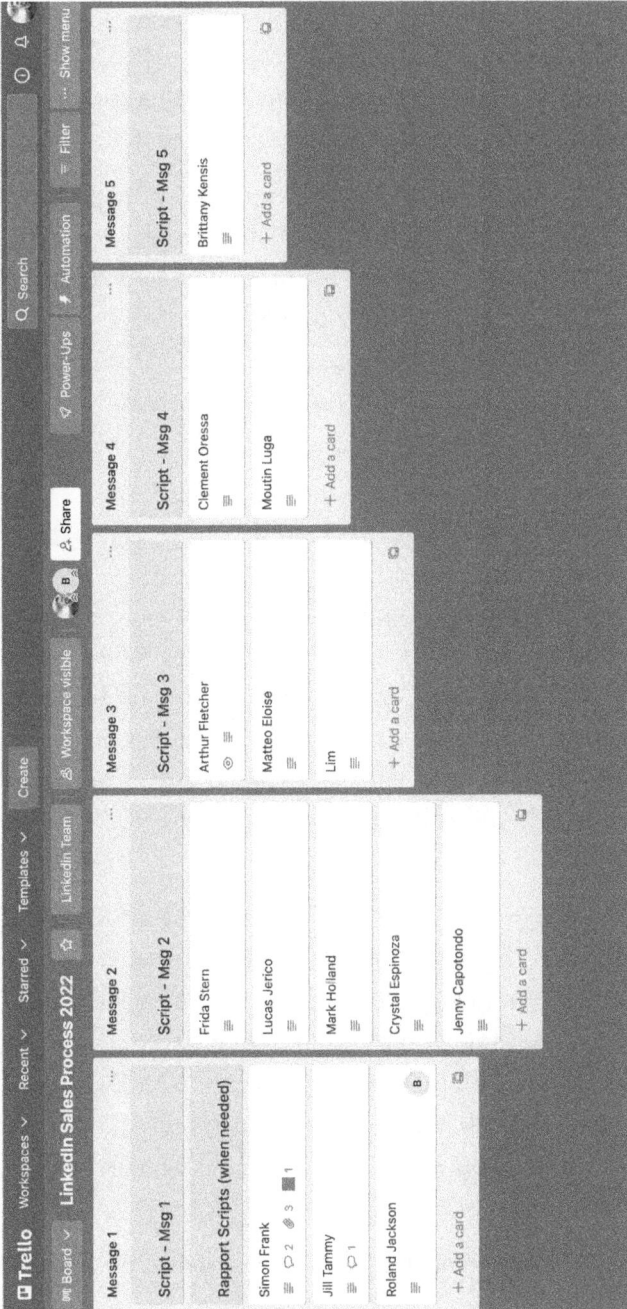

Image 3: Trello

And now you are ready to hand the keys of your LinkedIn, Facebook, TikTok, or Instagram accounts to a trusted assistant. I have two people working on my LinkedIn profile and one on Instagram. But I still check my inboxes a couple of times a week.

That's because as much as you plan ahead, your prospects can ask you something completely unrelated. So for those types of messages, we use an additional list in Trello called "Manager Follow-ups." When my team can't find a relevant reply to what the prospect wrote, they put the prospect's card in that list. I get a notification, then I check the notes and head over to LinkedIn to answer.

Showcasing Your Social Proof

Now let's get back to our testimonials, and let me ask you a question. When was the last time you bought something for more than $1,000 without doing some research first? If you are like most of us, you never did. By now, you should know that people are afraid of making the wrong purchase, so your goal is to address all their fears and doubts by getting testimonials that speak to those insecurities.

But if you let your clients talk freely about their experience of what you're offering, they'll rarely say exactly what your other prospects care about. I made the mistake of asking one of my first agency clients to record a short video testimonial without giving him any instructions. This is an excerpt from it. "Deniero is great at what he does, and he's so committed to my success that he even met me at a coffee shop on a Sunday morning to talk business once!"

That's all well and good, but he barely mentioned the fantastic new website, the increase in sales, and his social media growth. But that's not his fault at all. If I had given him some direction, he would have known what to focus on.

To avoid that, invite your happy client to a short video call and ask them questions that highlight the important points. If you are a videographer, for example, you can ask focused questions:

- When (and why) did you realize that you needed professional videos for your brand?

- How did professional videos affect your business and your sales?

- What is it like to work with us?

- Would you recommend us to other people, and if so, who would benefit from us the most?

Then get your team to replace your voice in the video with some music and have the questions pop up on screen. Add an intro, and you're done. Now you have a three-minute branded video testimonial that will help you close more deals.

But just like with your press, don't put your testimonials on an obscure page on your website. Show them often and make room for them in your marketing. In 2020, I had the privilege to interview the late entrepreneur Sam Bakhtiar, founder of The Camp Transformation Center, a gym franchise with over 100 locations. Sam used social proof everywhere. The Camp locations have lots of before-and-after photos of their clients near the entrance, and they also use testimonials on their ads. It's this upfront approach that puts people at ease. They think, "If it works for everyone, it will work for me too."

Now that you have lots of social proof, let's be tactical with it.

The last thing you want to do is send all your testimonials to your prospects right away. Instead, make sure you keep one of the best for the objection-handling stage of the call. Then, if necessary, play it on a screen share. And after your prospects see it, ask a couple of questions:

- Do you think that my client's circumstances were very different from yours?

- What's stopping you from getting the same results my other clients get?

We all love to think we're different, but we're not. One of my coaches is a personal trainer for busy fathers, and he has two kids himself. Once, he told me, "Deniero, you won't believe how many dads don't think my program applies to them because they have one child or three children, and I have two. Only when they see a testimonial with the same number of kids they have, do they buy."

Booking a Call and Closing the Deal

I want to wrap up this chapter by answering three questions about sales that I'm often asked.

First, "Should I prequalify my prospects before getting on the phone?"

Your time is important. So instead of spending days trying to convince a broke prospect to pay you $1,000, spend time attracting those who can afford to pay you $10,000.

But there's one exception to this rule. In the beginning, especially during your testing phase, you want to get on the phone with as many people as possible to practice your pitch and test your sales process. Then, when the machine is running smoothly, it's time to get picky. In fact, we'll cover a simple way to prequalify your prospects in the next chapter.

This takes me to the second question: "Should I have more than one sales call per prospect?" This depends on what you offer. I've tested the two methods with my agency and my coaching business, and they are both valuable.

The first method is the one-call close. Your prospect agrees to a longer call, and they know they might buy something. If there's no sale on the first call, you will set up a follow-up call.

The second method is the two-step close that includes a first 15-minute triage call to qualify the prospect and gather some information, and then a second longer call to show the offer and close the deal. And of course, if the deal doesn't go through, a third call.

The one-call close is perfect for standardized offers because the pitch won't change too much from prospect to prospect. But if you are offering a highly customized plan, you will need a triage call to gather information and put together a proposal.

Pick the one that works best for you, but remember to strike while the iron's hot. The more you let a prospect wait, the less interested they'll be.

Which brings us to the third question: "When a client says 'no,' should I try to close a deal on the spot or set a follow-up?" This is the age-old question that divides most salespeople. On one hand, the relationship builders will tell you that pressuring someone into buying might work in the moment, but not in the long run. On the other, the closers will swear by it and will justify the pressure by saying that they are acting in the prospect's best interest. But just as I said in the previous answer, every product is different, so you should tailor your approach accordingly.

When someone stays on a call with me to the end, it's because they want what I'm offering. And I'm not afraid to apply some pressure to help them get over their limiting beliefs and close on the spot.

But my team and I sell digital marketing and coaching services. If I were closing a $10 million solar panel installation contract, for example, I would likely take it slower.

CHAPTER 11

FUNNELS AND AUTOMATION

Trade Money for Time

Congratulations! You made it to the turning point. You've learned how to build your brand and make more money. Now it's time to automate, delegate, and free up your schedule. This chapter is all about putting your lead generation on autopilot.

As a digital marketing agency owner, I've spoken to well over 1,000 prospects over the years, but only a small percentage of them were prepared to advertise with us. Since we work on a revenue-sharing model, we have precise requirements that our prospects must meet. Let me tell you what they are so you can figure out if you are ready to advertise.

The first thing we look for is previous sales. If you have never sold your offer before, we wouldn't work with you. That's because no matter how great our ads are, the offer may just not convert.

Then we look at brand recognition. In other words, are you just another tiny goldfish in the pond, or are you a 10-pound koi? I'm not saying that you should only advertise if you are number one in your market. But if your business is very new and has little to no online presence other than the ads, you are fighting an uphill battle.

And last, we check your systems. Is your email marketing in place and up to date? Is your website fast and mobile-optimized? Do you have the tools and people to fulfill your offer? Do you have enough budget to pay for the ads?

I can't stress this enough: investing in ads before you've invested in the fundamentals is like waking up every morning and lighting cash on fire.

I know you are different, though. You're working on building a solid foundation, and you'll be ready to run ads soon. But should you try managing them on your own or hire a professional?

Given that your time is precious, unless you're planning on building a digital ad agency, you probably shouldn't waste time trying to master ads. Ad platforms are constantly evolving and new features pop in and out of existence like soap bubbles. If you want to run competitive campaigns, you're likely to spend more time testing and learning new features than working on your business. A task that is time consuming or technical, like marketing, needs to be outsourced ASAP.

Now you're ready to look for a marketing agency, but what type of ads should you run? To figure out where to start, ask yourself this question: "Is my market already looking for what I sell?" If the answer is "yes," start with search engine marketing. These are the sponsored listings you find at the top and bottom of a search result page on a site like Google or Bing. That's because you might as well pay to show up in front of people searching for your product.

But if you are trying to spark interest in what you are selling, you should begin with social media marketing. These are the paid posts you see when you scroll on social media platforms like Facebook and Instagram. When you advertise that way, you don't target your audience based on purchase intent, but by interest.

For example, if you are a dentist, you probably want to run a local Google Ads campaign to capture all the neighboring searches for fillings and teeth whitening. But if you're hosting a yoga retreat in Costa Rica, you're better off starting from Instagram and targeting yoga enthusiasts who also love to travel.

Funnels for Products, Services, and More

While you look for a marketer to run your ads, let's make sure that you're sending traffic to the right place. Too many business owners send traffic to a standard (boring) website and then wonder why they don't get many sales. Let me be very up-front about this. Don't send traffic to a regular website unless you have an e-commerce store or a platform like Expedia.

An average site has way too many options for your visitors. If someone lands on your page to learn about your consulting services, they could easily get sidetracked by your About page, and if they can't immediately find what they're looking for, they're gone in seconds!

So be clear about what you want your visitors to do, and instead send your traffic to a sales funnel that has that one objective. A funnel has no menu or different buttons to click on at the top. You can read text, watch videos, and move only in one direction. If you want visitors to book a sales call, have a video to pitch the call at the top, and place a Book a Call button underneath. If you want to sell a course, you can write the course outline, place some testimonials underneath, and the Buy Now button below.

It doesn't matter what you sell or who you sell to. You can even set up multiple funnels for different products or offerings within your business.

Let's use the dentist example again. You could run a campaign to your regular website and wait until someone calls you. Or you could pick three services and send traffic to three different funnels. For example, you could advertise teeth whitening, braces, and Invisalign. Each campaign will send traffic to a highly relevant page that explains why your practice is the best at that service. Then you could add one button to let your visitors book an in-person consultation, and you're done! You didn't distract your lead with irrelevant material. Instead, you grabbed them by the hand and took them directly through the buying process.

That's the beauty of having a truly automated lead-generation system. And once you start getting a good inflow of leads, you can even screen your prospects, so only the serious leads get to speak to your team.

After my team and I optimized the funnel copy and the ad targeting for my agency, we were getting about 60 calls a week, but many of them didn't qualify for the revenue-share service. So instead of sending visitors from the landing page directly to the calendar, we added a page in the middle with a conditional questionnaire.

In short, when people clicked on Book a Call, they first had to fill out a survey with questions regarding the size of their business, their ad budget, etc. Then, based on their answers, the automation directed them to the appropriate page. If their business was too small or they had a tiny ad budget, they were sent to a Thank You page that said, "Thanks for your interest; we'll get back to you once we have an opening." Then we nurtured the lead by sending them our newsletters. But if they had an established business and a reasonable ad budget, they were directed through to our sales team's calendar.

From that day on, we only got on the phone with highly qualified leads who could decide on the spot. That's the power of automation at its finest.

Offer Value Up Front

But you may be wondering, "What do I put on a landing page that will encourage people to book a call?" The truth is that it depends on what you are selling.

For example, if you are selling a quirky kitchen gadget with your funnel, you just need a good sales letter, a few good-quality photos and videos, and a couple of testimonials. But if you are a professional offering a service or selling a digital product, you need to provide value up front. This can be in the form of free training, a webinar, or an e-book. People are busier than ever, and they are too smart to sit through a 20-minute sales pitch. But they will take the time to watch a video or read a report if they think it could solve a problem they have, and they'll even give you their email! That's why these freebies are called lead magnets. Then if you do a good job at following up with newsletters and other touchpoints, you'll stay top of mind until they are ready to buy.

If you are on the fence between making a training video or writing an e-book (or something else altogether), let me give you some great news. The two are not mutually exclusive. You could write an e-book and then use it as a script to make a training video or vice versa. In fact, we always encourage our clients to use as many channels as possible. At one point, Bradley had a training video, e-books, webinars, reports, and audio content and was getting lots of leads with all of them. Some people like to sit down at a computer, while others want to learn while they're on the go. The aim of the game is to get your free material in the hands of as many people as possible.

When it comes to lead magnets, the key is to test different ones. Ron Mourra (IG: ronmourra), who is one of my coaches, is great at this strategy. He comes up with a new e-book or cheat sheet almost every season. For instance, he has "28 Clean-Eating Recipes to Make on The Grill" in the summer. Then in the winter, he has a "Meal Prep Guide,"[20] etc. He also has e-books and short, free courses based on age and the types of diets people follow. That allows him to target a wide range of prospects while still appearing very relevant.

That doesn't mean that you should spend all your time writing or filming new lead magnets. Remember that this is still part of your content strategy, so if you are already batching your videos, audio, and written posts, just take a couple of hours every three months to collect them into a larger free offer. Let me show you how.

Repurpose Your Marketing and Teaching Material

Start with being clear on what the lead magnet will be about. Let's say that you are a therapist helping young professionals deal with

---

[20] Ron Mourra, "Meal Prep Guide," accessed June 28, 2022, http://www. lean-fit-healthy.com/wp-content/uploads/2019/04/Lean-Fit-Healthy-Meal-prep-Guide-PDF-2019.pdf.

anxiety. First, break down all the possible challenges they could be facing (e.g., coping with a stressful job, fear of public speaking, anxiety during interviews). Then pick one issue and make it your new lead magnet topic. Now take a 30,000- foot view of all your content and pick the posts that best fit the lead magnet's theme.

Now, let's plan a free course.

> Title: Crush Interview Anxiety and Get Your Dream Job

> Lesson 1: Intro to the Problem (Go on camera and use one of your old blog posts as a script.)

> Lesson 2: How to Deal with Anxiety When It Arises (Take two or three highlights from your old YouTube videos and combine them.)

> Lesson 3: Daily Exercises to Overcome Anxiety (Go on camera and use a couple of your old infographics as an outline.)

> Lesson 4: Case Studies and Success Stories (Use your video testimonials and dig deeper into your clients' outcomes.)

But why would someone be attracted to a lead magnet if they can find the same information on your social media accounts?

It's a good question. But in fact, people are willing to pay ridiculous amounts of money for convenience when buying information, even when that knowledge could have been free. Reading books at a public library is free, but many people buy books for $30 apiece just because they can read them when they have time. And what about private fitness classes? Most exercise routines can be found for free on YouTube, but many people will pay to get a tailored fitness experience, even though the underlying information is the same.

You have done the work of assembling your free content into an organized manual to help someone with a specific problem. And that's the convenience we are talking about. But if you are still worried about sharing too much, to the point of losing sales, then let's look at what Russell Brunson has to say about it in his book *Expert Secrets*.

Russell's advice is to use your free content to share strategies, but not tactics—strategies being the high-level plans and tactics being the detailed step-by-step processes.[21] If you were a mountain guide, for example, you would share the different routes to go from point A to point B and all the stops in between, but you wouldn't show the details of how you get past every obstacle.

If your content is high-level and not customized, you can share it for free, but if it's detailed, tailored to your clients' needs, convenient, and organized to solve a specific problem, you should save it for your high-ticket offering.

Take a look at figure 9, and try to apply it to your business.

---

[21] Russell Brunson, *Expert Secrets* (Carlsbad: Hay House, 2020).

DONE FOR YOU SERVICE
(NO NEED FOR KNOWLEDGE)

CUSTOM-MADE TACTICS,
STRATEGIES + KNOWLEDGE

ALREADY-MADE
TACTICS, STRATEGIES +
KNOWLEDGE

SERVICE

CONSULTING/COACHING

PAID COURSES

LEAD MAGNETS + WEBINARS

SOCIAL MEDIA POSTS, PODCAST +
YOUTUBE VIDEOS

ORGANIZED STRATEGIES
AND KNOWLEDGE

UNORGANIZED
STRATEGIES AND
KNOWLEDGE

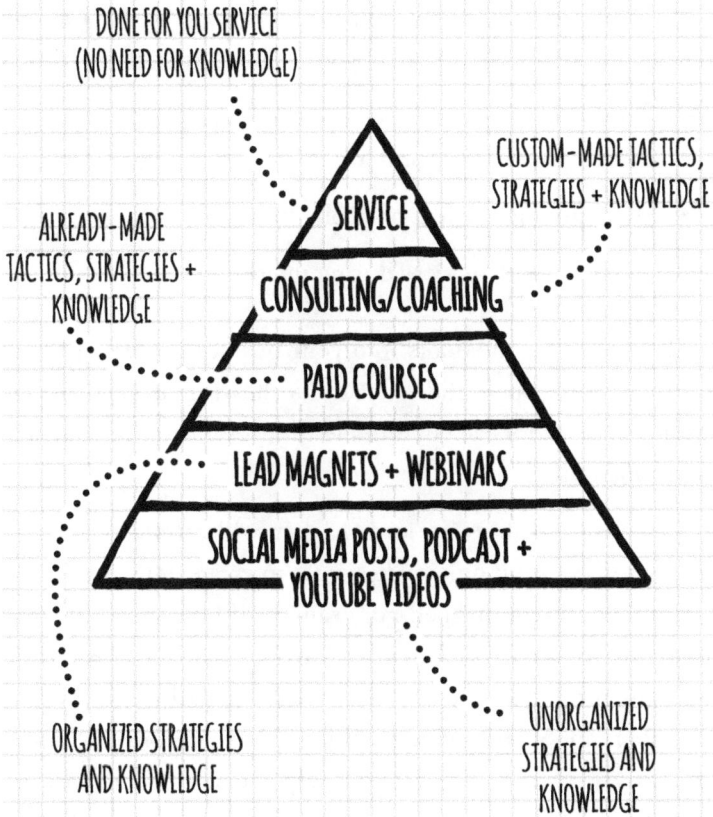

Figure 9: Information Pyramid

SMART BUSINESS, BETTER YOU

Different Ways to Get Clients in the Door

Before we move on to the team-building section of the book, let's have a final look at how you can use lead magnets to maximize your lead generation.

Let's imagine again that you are a therapist helping young professionals with anxiety, and you finally have all three lead magnets:

- Coping with a stressful job

- Conquering the fear of public speaking

- Dealing with anxiety during interviews

These are now the doors into your business, so you'd better keep them wide open and keep traffic flowing at all times by building a funnel for each one and letting your team (or your ads) drive traffic to them.

As I mentioned, every lead magnet will attract a different type of prospect, so it only makes sense to create email sequences relevant to each lead magnet. For example, if I give you my email in exchange for the Crush Interview Anxiety and Get Your Dream Job mini-course, I'd expect to receive a few emails regarding the same topic, not about public speaking. So when someone enters your ecosystem from one funnel, keep emails specific to their interests for the first couple of weeks, and only later start sending them the general newsletter.

That may seem like a small deal, but it's a game-changer because you can target specific subsections of a niche simply by deploying new lead magnets.

For example, if you are a business consultant for dental

practices, you could promote a free report called *Open Your First Dental Practice Fast* to target new dentists. But you could also promote another, titled *Growing Your Multilocation Dental Group* to attract larger businesses.

Now, let's not forget why you are creating all these lead magnets. The goal is to get your prospects invested enough in the process to get started and possibly come back to you for help. So to maximize your chances of turning them into clients, you need to step up your call-to-action game, or in other words, ask for their business.

If you have a low-ticket offering (up to $1,000), you can sell right from your emails and lead magnets, but for anything over $1,000, aim to get prospects on a call to move them closer to the purchase. You can write things like "If you found this report useful and want to know how to speed up the process, let's get on a quick call!" or "This month we are offering 10 free consultation calls to the members of our list—book yours now!"

SECTION 4

BUILD YOUR TEAM

CHAPTER 12

MAPPING OUT YOUR TEAM

Create a Map of the Roles You Need

N ow that you know how to get leads and turn them into sales, let's put our CEO hats on and build your team. The majority of those who start an online business don't make it all the way. They either stay small and hire one assistant at most or give up altogether. But you are different. Not only are you growing your income, but you're also creating the systems that will free you up from your time-vampire business.

Our first exercise comes straight from Chris Ducker's book *Virtual Freedom*.[22] Divide a sheet of paper into three columns, and list the following sets of tasks: things you don't like doing, things that you can't do, and things you shouldn't do. Here's what my list looks like.

---

[22] Chris Ducker, *Virtual Freedom: How to Work with Virtual Staff to Buy More Time, Become More Productive, and Build Your Dream Business* (Dallas: BenBella Books, 2014).

Things I Don't Like Doing:	Things That I Can't Do:	Things That I Shouldn't Do:
• post on social media	• write code	• edit my podcast
• do general research	• design graphics	• handle customer support
• look for podcast guests	• file taxes	• update the company's websites
• do outreach on LinkedIn and Instagram	• edit videos	• do keyword research for my content
• send invoices		• manage my clients' ad accounts
• troubleshoot apps and software		• make sales calls for my ad agency
• set up automation tools		
• manage operations		

Now take a look at your list. It will show you who you need to hire.

When you build a team from scratch, the first tasks you need to outsource are those you don't know how to do yourself. That's because if you don't delegate that work to a professional, your systems and your brand image won't be on par with your competitors. So, please stop launching cookie-cutter websites or designing ugly banners. Stop trying to learn new peripheral skills. Instead, focus on getting better at your own craft and be confident in outsourcing the rest.

Once you take care of those items, it's time to look at things that you shouldn't do. These are sneaky tasks because you'll catch yourself thinking, "I'm just going to do it myself. It'll only take me 10 minutes anyway." However, be mindful of what you allow yourself to do. For example, I know how to edit a podcast, but I shouldn't be spending two hours a week cutting and pasting audio files. I also know how to do keyword research and manage ads, but if I entered that rabbit hole, I'd be in it for days. So, to avoid that, hire team members to take care of those roles, which will leave you time to concentrate on your essential tasks.

And finally, delegate the work you don't like to do. If you don't like selling, for example, this is the stage where you can hire a salesperson. You earned it! Up to this point, you had to work daily on your revenue-generating tasks and the upkeep of your business. But the time has come to choose how much you want to work and what you want to work on.

Decide How Many People You Need

A big factor in deciding how big your team will be is your revenue. As a rule of thumb, if you are selling a service or a digital product (e.g., consulting, accounting, digital marketing, video editing), you should spend about a third of your revenue on labor. That's why you must command higher prices, because if you don't, you'll have to choose between hiring inexperienced people or doing the work yourself.

Do you remember my client Liam who now lives his dream lifestyle in Vancouver? When he was scaling his agency, he looked at recurring revenue at the end of every month and allocated a third of it to hire new contractors. In the beginning, he could only afford to outsource part of the client work and the odd one-off task. But as his reputation grew, and he started charging more, he quickly added more team members and was nearly able to automate the entire thing.

Follow the same process, and you will be free from your day-to-day work faster than you think. But what if your workload fluctuates a lot? Should you still invest in a team? The answer is "yes." You'll need to acquire management skills sooner or later, so why not go through the learning phase when your business is relatively small? Hire away! Make your mistakes as a leader. They won't cost you too much now.

When I first put my team together, I could have won the award for being the most unreliable manager. I missed an average of two meetings out of every five. When my team messaged me, it'd take me a few days to answer. My excuse was that I was busy. Then when I messaged them, I'd be annoyed if they didn't reply within an hour. Of course, everyone quit on me in less than 90 days. That was my first leadership lesson: lead by example, because no one will care about your business more than you do.

But things changed quickly after that. That's when I became obsessed with learning how to look for and hire the right talent. Back then, I could only afford to hire contractors by the hour, but I had issues with their availability, so I ran hundreds of interviews and developed a color-coding system to keep track of the best candidates and how much notice they needed to start working. Since then, I have never run out of talent for any positions.

One of the biggest mistakes that small-business owners make is that they don't run enough interviews, so they settle for the best of four or five candidates. Or, even worse, they don't fire an underperforming team member because they'd rather not go through the hassle of finding someone else. In fact, if you want to grow faster than your competition, run more interviews and raise your standards with your team. That will give you the confidence to replace employees who are not performing.

Decide on the Types of Contracts You Can Offer

Now let's look at different contract options. These are the most common types:

- One-off contract work

- Outsourcing agency (full-time or part-time)

- Direct hiring (full-time or part-time)

One-off contract work

If you need a new website, for example, you don't need to hire a full-time web developer, so you'd hire a contractor to take care of that one project. This is a great working arrangement for any new business because it allows you to be flexible with your budget. The drawback, though, is that contractors have many clients, and your work is not any more important than the rest. As a result, you may find yourself waiting a long time for something that should only take a couple of hours. So as soon as your workload increases, move away from this model.

Outsourcing agencies (full-time or part-time)

These are a fantastic alternative to hiring full-time or part-time employees because they do the heavy lifting for you. They will often assign you a qualified and prescreened assistant, and in some cases, they will train them too. Then if something happens (e.g., the assistant gets sick, or they are not a good fit), the agency will replace them with a new person. This type of convenience comes at a steep price, though. On average, outsourcing agencies charge almost double what you would pay if you hired a staff member directly. So before hiring through an agency, ask yourself how much you value this kind of peace of mind.

Direct hiring (full-time or part-time)

This is the optimal working arrangement for assigning daily, weekly, and monthly revolving tasks. My full-time team members work on lead generation, social media management, video editing, graphic design, digital ads management, and admin. And since they work with me every day, I get to set regular meetings, and the turnaround time on the work is much faster.

The only problem with hiring a full-time staff member arises if your revenue fluctuates too much. So if you don't have enough work to delegate, hold off from hiring full-time and opt for a task-based contract instead.

Now let's look at the difference between task-based and role-based hiring.

Hire for the Task or for the Role

You're almost ready to be a remote CEO. But before you get there, we need to iron out the last details.

First, you need to decide whether you are hiring for the task or for the role—that will dictate whether you hire for a couple of hours a week or on a full-time or part-time basis. It's the difference between hiring a designer who only designs a few social media posts a week or a graphic designer who takes care of all your design needs. These are not like the contractors who work on one-off tasks, but since the work is very repetitive, avoid hiring a full-time person for it as they will get tired of the job quickly.

My client Phil started using task-based hiring when scaling his Amazon pay-per-click (PPC) agency. As he grew, he found that the most time-consuming tasks in his business were keyword research and optimization. So he first hired two full-time marketers, but he soon noticed a drop in morale due to them working on these very repetitive tasks. And that's when he switched to task-based hiring and hired six people, who each worked seven hours per week.

This was a more flexible way to meet demand, but it also prevented low morale from spreading in the company due to job dissatisfaction.

So let's look at the most common work you can outsource in a task-based fashion:

- Social media post design
- Podcast editing
- Video editing for social media and YouTube
- Bookkeeping
- Social media marketing
- Search engine marketing
- Copywriting

If you look at the list above, you'll notice that all these tasks require specialized knowledge. So, instead of hiring a general assistant to take care of them, you should rely on a specialized individual for each job.

On the other hand, general virtual assistants (GVAs) are great for nonspecialized work. As long as you train them well, they'll take care of various tasks across different platforms. Here are some examples of nonspecialized tasks:

- Social media community engagement

- LinkedIn or Instagram outreach

- Posting on social media, podcasts, or YouTube

- Managing email inboxes and replying to inquiries

- Researching and putting together reports

- Uploading blog posts to your site

- Managing your email-marketing software

GVAs are considered role-based hires because they are either part-time or full-time, and they work on many projects simultaneously. In contrast, role-based positions that take care of specialized work are operations managers, graphic designers, and project managers, among others.

Take a look at figure 10 to see the pros and cons of hiring for the task and hiring for the role.

TASK-BASED

- CONTRACTORS WITH AN ONGOING CONTRACT
- AGENCIES
- WORKING LESS THAN 15 HOURS A WEEK

PROS
- FLEXIBILITY
- FOCUS

CONS
- NOT INVOLVED IN THE BUSINESS
- SLOWER COMMUNICATION
- SLOWER TURNAROUND

ROLE-BASED

- FULL TIME OR PART TIME ROLE
- THEY ONLY WORK WITH YOU AND MAXIMUM ONE MORE BUSINESS

PROS
- PERFECT TO BUILD CULTURE
- QUICK COMMUNICATION
- CARE ABOUT THE BUSINESS

CONS
- MAY BE TOO EXPENSIVE IN THE BEGINNING

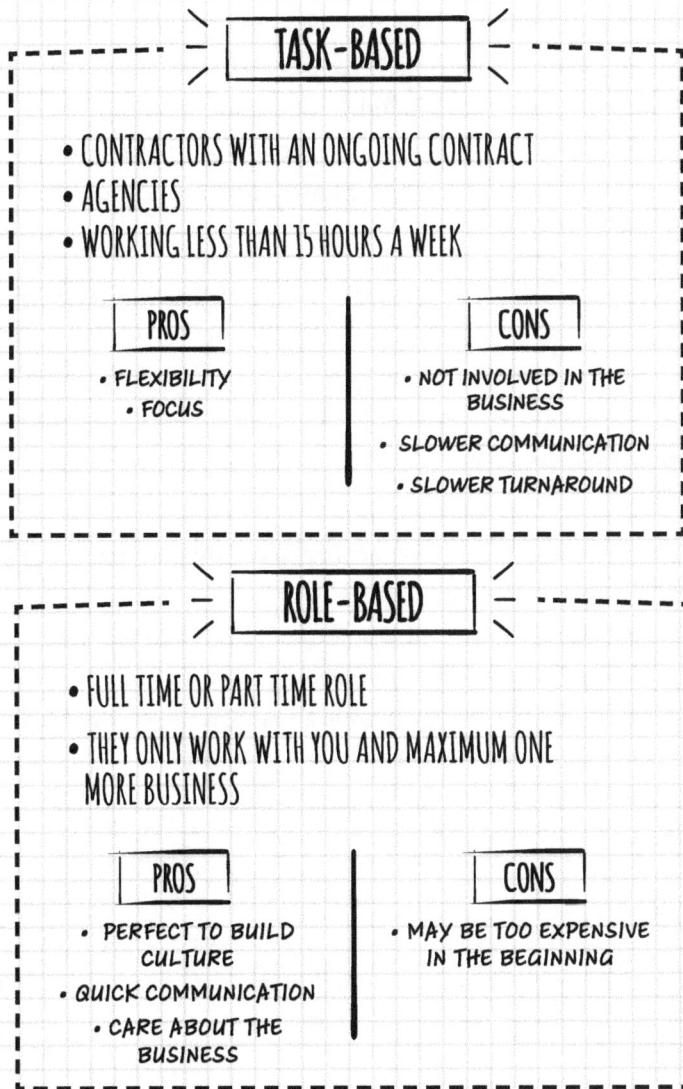

Figure 10: Pros and Cons of Hiring for the Task and Hiring for the Role

Know When to Hire or Do Your Job Yourself

And at last, let's look at the tasks that you should retain control over for as long as you can. Of course, every business is different, and every entrepreneur should decide how much they want to work. But as a rule, when you are building a lifestyle business, the things you should not delegate are planning, networking, and building culture.

This is *your* lifestyle business, and as we discussed in chapter 3, all the company's goals need to be aligned with your vision and values if you're to be successful. That's why you should do the planning. If you want to be more efficient at it, ask your assistant to research the relevant topics and send you an executive summary.

Networking should also be a DIY task, especially if you are building a personal brand. That's because you never know where your next opportunity will come from. For example, in chapter 2 I told you about being introduced to a booking agent who put my podcast on the map. It all came about because he and I had an impromptu conversation that led to podcasting.

And third, hold tight to culture-building for as long as you can. Think of building and maintaining your business culture as being the host of your own event. You decide the dress code, the theme, and what the party will be like. You want to make sure to hire (or "invite") people who work well together. And it's also your responsibility to maintain that balance in the long run.

For every other task, the formula we use at The Remote CEO is simple. First, look at how many hours you work every week, and assign a dollar amount to your time. At this point in my life, I work an average of 15 hours per week, and based on my current rates, I value my time at $1,000 per hour.

If my schedule is complete, I make sure that I don't work on anything that I can outsource for less than that amount. But if I still have some free time, I start working on the highest-valued task under $1,000 per hour.

There is a caveat, though. Not all tasks will instantly generate revenue. For example, I've been writing this book for a month, and I have invested close to 200 hours in it already. But I haven't made $200,000 from it yet. Soon, though, the book will elevate my brand and help me reach a much wider audience, and that will likely be worth a lot more than $200,000.

If you want to grow your business faster, you need to balance your schedule between tasks that generate instant revenue and those that build your brand and improve your systems. Unfortunately, many entrepreneurs fail to grow because they don't manage this balance effectively. They spend too little time either on revenue-generating tasks or on "optimizing the machine."

Bradley knows this all too well. When he first started in real estate, he was running around from showing to showing, competing with other real estate professionals. Then he decided to allocate a few hours a week to starting his podcast, content creation, and brand building. To the untrained eye, Bradley was not actively growing his business. But after a couple of years of optimizing his messaging and his systems, he was able to turn his small show into the most recognized podcast in his market. Some things are just not meant to be outsourced.

CHAPTER 13

HIRING YOUR TEAM

Create a Big Pool of Candidates

A few years ago, when I was running a seminar at a government-funded agency, I asked the group, "What's the worst staffing mistake you could make?"

Almost everyone answered, "Hiring too many people and not having enough work to give them." In fact, the correct answer is the opposite.

Let's pretend that you own a restaurant, and you have to pick one of the two following scenarios.

1. Schedule 10 servers on a Wednesday and only get two tables for the night.

2. Schedule two servers on a Saturday and have your restaurant fully booked.

The answer should be simple. Sure, you may lose $1,000 in wages in the first scenario, but in the second, the repercussions will be worse and last a lot longer. Think of all the unhappy customers who will never come back and will tell their friends about their horrible experience.

In the last chapter, I told you about my fear of running out of talent and how it pushed me to create a system to keep track of multiple candidates. Such a system is not only good for improving the quality of the talent you hire, but it also helps you avoid situations like scenario 2 above.

What if, as that restaurant owner, you had access to a long list of on-call servers whom you could contact any time you needed more help? Would you still make the same staffing mistakes? Probably not.

In my third year in business with my agency, I launched a promotion to offer new, custom Shopify stores to those who signed up for our ad package. But inconveniently enough, our web developer quit, and I was left with seven clients waiting for their sites. Worst of all, since we promised that we'd run ads straight to their new sites, I couldn't even start their ad campaigns.

Fortunately, I had already been working on my handy staffing document, and I quickly contacted three developers I had previously interviewed. One of them was ready to start working immediately, so we averted a crisis in less than five minutes.

Let me stress that this was not a last-minute replacement I had to settle for. The new hire was one of the many candidates I had interviewed in the past, and I had really liked. But since I could only use one person at that time, I hadn't hired him earlier.

It's not a coincidence that all the successful organizations I've worked for were constantly running interviews (sometimes too many—we'll talk about that soon.) It didn't matter if they were expanding or not. They knew that employees would come and go and that honest and motivated talent was hard to come by.

Hire Based on Hands-On Experience

I want to clarify that when I refer to "talent," I am not only talking about candidates with a college education. I know I'm going to ruffle some feathers, but I don't consider formal education, like a degree, essential to business success. In fact, in our team of 20 people, only a few have a degree.

I have a four-year degree in international business plus a business management diploma, and I can tell you that I have applied very little information from my school years in my work. Some of that knowledge is plain outdated, while I don't even remember the rest.

But the reason why I'm successful is that I keep on studying on my own—I read books, I see a coach, I practice my craft, and I learn from my mistakes. And those are the same qualities that I look for in my staff. I'd hire a lifelong learner with hands-on experience over a candidate with just a degree any day.

Of course, formal education is essential for many professions that require standardized abilities and knowledge. For example, I'm sure you wouldn't want a surgeon without formal medical education. But when I help my clients build their online business, most of them prioritize hiring problem-solvers and self-starters. They are not looking for standardized knowledge.

When we scaled our digital marketing agency, we had a serious need for Facebook and Google marketers. The platforms were (and still are) evolving at record speed, and our primary target was finding someone with a very recent, proven track record.

To put this into perspective, this was in 2018, when Facebook was dealing with significant privacy issues, and the platform was getting rid of several targeting parameters every month. So, if you ran a successful Facebook Ads campaign just six months before that time, chances were you had used some settings that were now obsolete.

But when you're building an online business, almost all tools are ever changing. From email marketing to social media and funnels, your staff should constantly be experimenting with new approaches and take time to master each new software version.

Refresher courses can be useful, but they are not the only way to acquire new knowledge. Benchmarking your successful competitors is also an extremely efficient way to learn what's working now. And it has become such a crucial phase in running an online business that Russell Brunson came up with a new term for it: "funnel hacking." Or in other words, reverse-engineering other successful funnels to find out what makes them successful. This, however, doesn't mean that you need to copy others blindly. When funnel hacking, keep your audience and your product in mind, keep testing, and make sure that your personal and your brand's values align with any of the tactics you roll out.

Hiring for an online business has a lot more to do with attitude and recent results than anything else. So, if you are coming from a traditional industry, make sure to adjust your recruiting parameters to fit these new standards.

To give you a quick example, these are my two most common questions in interviews:

1. What's your biggest and most recent success?

2. When was the last time you took a refresher course on [enter topic]?

Create Compelling Job Postings

When I was starting my corporate career, I'd apply for jobs on online portals, where you could see the number of applicants for each role: "1,450 people applied for this position." Even with the help of a résumé scanner, can you imagine having to check hundreds of applications? The idea is that more applications lead to more interviews, but at what cost?

Earlier in the chapter, I noted that successful businesses tend to run many interviews but that they could do a better job of prescreening candidates.

Let me give you an example of the average job posting you can find on a portal. "XYZ Inc. is looking to hire a visionary sales expert to be part of a dynamic and positive team. This is a unique opportunity to join an amazing company and work on a special project that will give you unlimited earning potential."

Is this company based in Utopia? No wonder job postings like this are flooded with applicants. The issue is not the number of applicants, though; it's the quality.

But there's a better way. If you only want to speak to motivated people ready to get out of their comfort zone, just be up-front with them. For example, here's an excerpt from an operations manager's job description that I posted on an employment site.

Hiring an Operations Manager for a Challenging and Demanding Role

We're looking for a self-starter who can constantly excel unsupervised. We run a digital marketing agency.

Our team members and clients work across 15 time zones, so you may be asked to work unconventional hours twice a week.

We also hire several marketers each month, so on top of your regular operations management duties, you'll be required to help us onboard new staff and bring them up to speed with their projects.

Our industry is evolving fast, and we only hire life-long learners, so we expect all our staff members to keep their knowledge up to date by taking monthly refresher courses outside of working hours.

This is not a regular operations management job. On top of your regular duties, you're required to think of creative ways to increase profit margins while maintaining high customer service standards.

We also don't like mistakes, and our motto is "Hire slow, fire fast," so if you don't think you can maintain these standards on an ongoing basis, you are not a good fit, and that's okay!

If, after reading this, you are excited to know more, here's what you get from us:

- *Monthly group mentorship calls with our CEO*

- *Profit-sharing on all revenue-generating activities outside of your job description*

- *Flexible schedule outside of meeting times*

In seven days we received only 20 applications with the job posting above. But out of those, 17 were interview material. And even though we only hired one person for that role, we kept 13 in our candidate database and ended up recruiting five of them at a later time.

Setting the right expectations during the hiring process is like writing marketing copy about your offering. The more you niche down, the more you exclude possible buyers. But every time your messaging repels one person, it creates a stronger connection with those who are a good fit.

Figure 11 gives you a visual representation of what happens with both approaches.

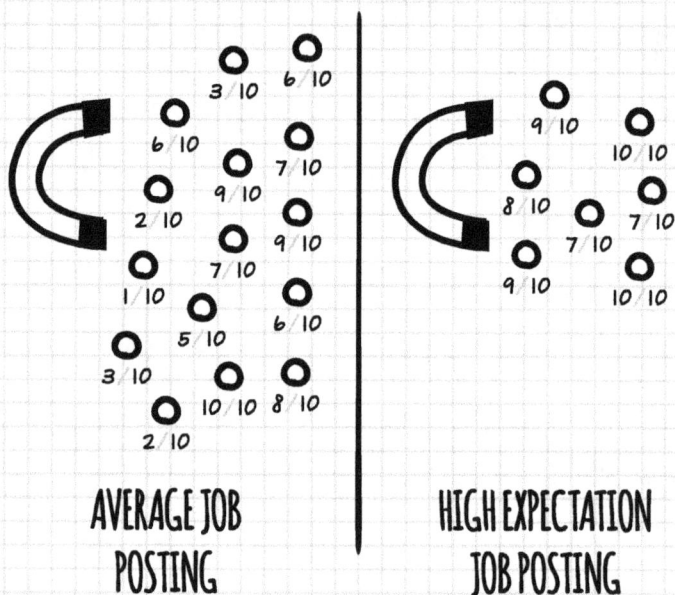

AVERAGE JOB POSTING

HIGH EXPECTATION JOB POSTING

HIGH EXPECTATION JOB POSTINGS PRE-SCREEN YOUR CANDIDATES AND ONLY GET YOU TO SPEAK WITH MOTIVATED HIGH ACHIEVERS

Figure 11: Setting the Right Expectations in Job Offerings

Tap into Your Network

Another great way to discover and hire good talent is to tap into your network. But that doesn't mean that you should hire based on who you know. Your network is not a single layer of connections. Every person you have networked with may know someone who could be a good match for the position you're looking to fill. So reach out to them, and ask if they know anyone who fits your criteria.

Earlier in the chapter, I told you that what's important is not the number of job applicants but the quality. And the same rule applies to your network. You should cultivate meaningful relationships with other entrepreneurs and executives and strive to give more value than you ask for. Then, when you are looking to hire your next marketer or salesperson, you're just one message away from connecting with a potential hire. That's because a warm introduction from someone you respect is the best referral you can get.

But what if, when you're starting out, you don't know any entrepreneurs or executives? We already covered this in chapter 4, but let me remind you of a couple of ways you can build your network fast.

First, look for in-person events in your industry. For example, if you are a lawyer, find meet-ups for legal professionals, and invest your time and money into developing connections. If you are operating on a tight budget, look for virtual meet-ups that offer access to a Facebook group or other networking opportunities. That way, you can learn from an expert panel and meet the attendees afterward.

Alternatively, get a coach. In the past four years, I asked my coaches for (and received) warm intros that resulted in me hiring five salespeople, one Facebook marketer, one podcast agent to represent me, one YouTube marketer, one copywriter, and one funnel expert. That's 10 people, and they're still working with me. And as a coach myself, I share my network with all my clients, making it easier for them to assemble an A+ team.

But this doesn't mean that you should never look for talent yourself. Think of asking for an introduction as going out to eat a four-course meal at a fancy restaurant, and think of finding your own candidates as making your dinner at home.

An introduction is a done-for-you connection, but although it's typically good quality, it's often not scalable. Conversely, looking for talent on a job site requires you to do the work, but as long as you know what you're doing, you can hire as many suitable candidates as you want.

In fact, I only ask for introductions when I am looking to fill revenue-generating roles. That's because those jobs require the most recent hands-on experience. But when we're hiring for positions like designers, operations managers, customer service reps, and social media managers, we look for talent ourselves.

Hire Based on Time Zone Needs and Budget

One of the perks of being a remote CEO is that you get to choose where to operate from. You could be lying on a beach in Bali while your Bulgarian team is helping you run your consulting business in the United States. Or you could be in the U.S. while your team in the Philippines helps you onboard clients in the UK. So be mindful of time zones in the locations where you are looking for talent.

My wife and I relocated to Italy, six hours ahead of New York and nine hours ahead of L.A. And since most of my clients are in North America, I only work between 1 p.m. and 6:30 p.m.

Then my admin and operations team members are in Europe, India, and the Philippines, which are between one and six hours ahead of me. So that makes it easy for me to work with them after lunch.

And last, my customer-facing team members are in the U.S. That way, we maximize their ability to speak to our prospects and clients.

See, the goal is not to look for the cheapest hourly rates—it's about thinking strategically. For example, Bradley was working with talent in eastern Europe, but after a few years, he opted to hire locally because he needed help managing his client relationships in person. But if he didn't need in-person interactions, he could have looked for a native English speaker elsewhere.

Let me show the extent to which you can leverage time zones when you think creatively.

We talked about Phil when I showed you how to use task-based hiring. But what I didn't tell you is that once he had scaled his Amazon PPC agency, he realized that his clients also needed help dealing with Amazon customer service. If you've ever sold on Amazon, you know that something as simple as fixing a minor inventory issue can take five hours on the phone, four of which you're on hold (yes, really!).

With our help, he assembled a 24-hour tech support team by hiring three customer service reps who worked eight-hour shifts in different time zones. When one ended their workday, another would get started. Then he added one more person and set up weekend shifts to turn it into a 24/7 operation.

By now you should know how to plan the layout of your team based on what you want your lifestyle and business to look like. So let's look at how to manage that team.

CHAPTER 14

MANAGING YOUR TEAM

The Micromanagement Paradox

I f you are good at managing and motivating people, you can truly get your business running on autopilot.

One question that always pops up on our coaching calls is "Should I be a friendly manager, or should I be hard with my staff?"

The short answer is that being a compassionate and helpful manager leads to better employee morale and culture and ultimately increases productivity. But just being nice is not going to cut it. Your team needs a leader, not a friend.

Between my own mistakes and those of my clients, I could write an entire book on the pros and cons of different management styles, but instead, let's use Douglas McGregor's management theories, developed during the 1950s and 1960s, to visualize the two main archetypes.[23]

---

[23] John J. Morse and Jay W. Lorsch, "Beyond Theory Y," *Harvard Business Review*, May 1970, https://hbr.org/1970/05/beyond-theory-y.

The first are theory-X managers. They are controlling, pessimistic, and believe their staff members don't like their jobs. Although they reward hard work, they often use negative reinforcement to get their team to operate more efficiently.

The second are theory-Y managers. They are trusting, believe that people can enjoy their work, and motivate and lead by example. They let their staff make decisions and are more flexible since they place more emphasis on the results than the process.

Although theory-X is an outdated management style (especially in the online business world), some of its practices, when applied with empathy, can be very effective.

Take time trackers, for example. When I was first introduced to them, I hated the idea. Just the thought of timing my team made me feel like a 19th-century factory supervisor, but after taking a closer look, I fell in love with the idea.

Using a time tracker when you introduce a new task to your employees is the opposite of micromanaging. In fact, you are providing your team with clear metrics they can use to manage their own time better.

Let's pretend that you are launching a podcast, and you just hired an audio editor. You don't know how big the project is, so you ask your editor to track the time it takes them to complete one episode. When they finish and give you the report, you then have a benchmark that you can use to plan your podcasting timelines and budget going forward. Now imagine you did this with every task in your business.

You'll soon have a crystal clear picture of all your systems, and you'll never have to use a timer twice for the same task.

Another divisive topic is team meetings. Some companies

have way too many, while others avoid them at all costs. In fact, after interviewing hundreds of entrepreneurs for my podcast, I realized that many of them prefer to communicate through messaging apps, especially if they run asynchronous remote teams.

But even though my team works across 15 time zones, I like to speak to them every day. That's because I learned from my first sales jobs that a quick pump-up meeting can change your entire team's workday. Our daily meetings involve a concise agenda that allows us to cover everything in less than 10 minutes. The frequency of the meetings lets my team know they are not alone, while the brevity of the calls shows them that I respect their time and ability to work independently.

Regardless of what management style you lean toward, make sure it matches your brand. My coaching business, for example, is all about building your perfect lifestyle and working smart, so aside from mandatory meetings and sales calls, my team chooses when to work and what to work on. Your employees are the ones exposed to your brand the most, so if your brand messaging doesn't match the way you act around them, you'll foster a toxic environment.

Psychometric Assessments

Your job as a remote CEO is not to convince people to work for you but to recruit those already in line with how you run your business. Managing shouldn't feel like herding cats. That's particularly true when you operate remotely because once you hire your staff, your interactions with them are limited to calls and messages.

Some workers thrive in organized environments and love

working with colleagues, while others prefer working on their own with little supervision. Your goal as a manager is to find out what people are like and match them with the right type of job.

One of the biggest mistakes I made when I started my business was to hire an old colleague from my previous sales role. At that corporate job, he was a fantastic closer. He showed up early at the office and was our team's cheerleader. But when he started working alone from home with no supervision, I barely recognized him. He missed meetings, finished projects late, and the quality of his work was often below par. When we finally had a heart-to-heart conversation, he confessed that he hated working from home and that he was already looking for an in-person role elsewhere.

So, if it's not only excellence that you are looking for in a candidate, how do you measure compatibility? The answer is psychometric assessments.

I'd known about these self-assessments since college, but it wasn't until I read the book *Principles* by billionaire investor Ray Dalio that I incorporated them into my hiring process.[24] To my amazement, I made several hiring decisions against my instinct, and they all turned out to be on point. That's because these assessments shine a light on several variables that a typical interview can't predict.

For example, if you are trying to find out if someone is detail oriented, you could ask them during an interview, but they will probably give you the answer you want to hear, not the truth. And just like attention to detail, there are plenty more indicators that a psychometric assessment can reveal about a candidate:

- What motivates them?

---

[24] Ray Dalio, *Principles* (New York: Simon & Schuster, 2017).

- How do they deal with uncertainty?

- How do they cope with negative feedback?

- Do they prefer working alone or in a group?

- Can they work on repetitive tasks, or do they get bored quickly?

- Do they always need instructions, or can they make their own decisions?

- Are they just good workers, or could they evolve into a manager role?

In the beginning, you may be overwhelmed by the number of assessments available. We've used the Myers-Briggs Type Indicator, stratified systems theory, and the HEXACO-PI-R, to mention a few. But if you want to dip your toe in the water, start with a free test at 16personalities.com, which is a modification of the Myers-Briggs Type Indicator.

Regardless of which assessments you use, make sure to run at least two good interviews—one before the test and one after. That way you can combine the test results with your findings and build a clear picture of your candidate. As Dalio points out, "If I had to choose between just the assessments or just traditional job interviews to get at what people are like, I would choose the assessments. Fortunately, we don't have to make that choice."[25]

In my experience, new remote CEOs tend to oversimplify the hiring process hoping that things will work out in the end, so beware of that type of thinking before it starts to drive your hiring decisions. Dalio also states that "getting the right people in the

---

[25] Ray Dalio, "If I had to choose …," Twitter, April 21, 2021, https://twitter.com/RayDalio/status/1384946112386191363.

right roles in support of your goal is the key to succeeding at whatever you choose to accomplish." So when you're choosing your next team members, always keep compatibility front of mind.

The Advancing Personality

Now let's switch gears and talk about you—not your management style, not your strategic hiring, but just the way you act around people. That's because no matter how many tools or how much insight you have, you still have to be the kind of leader people want to work for.

And to find out the secret sauce, I'm going to take you back to 1910, to a book that has changed millions of lives: *The Science of Getting Rich* by Wallace D. Wattles.[26]

If you are not into woo-woo material, we're on the same page. In fact, although part of the teachings of this book were featured on Rhonda Byrne's documentary *The Secret*, (which is, in my opinion, an incomplete representation of what it takes to create the life you want, since it doesn't take into account one important factor: taking massive action!), *The Science of Getting Rich* is based on timeless psychological and sociological rules.[27]

Without getting into the wealth-building part of the book, let me share with you what Wallace D. Wattles has to say about dealing with others.

"All human activities are based on the desire for increase; people are seeking more food, more clothes, better shelter, more

---

[26] Wallace D. Wattles, *The Science of Getting Rich* (Holyoke: Elizabeth Towne, 1910).

[27] *The Secret*, directed by Drew Heriot (Melbourne: Prime Time Productions, 2006), 91 mins.

luxury, more beauty, more knowledge, more pleasure—increase in something, more life. [...] And because it is the deepest instinct of their natures, all men and women are attracted to [those] who can give them more of the means of life. [...] You are a creative center, from which increase is given off to all. Be sure of this, and convey assurance of [that] fact to every man, woman, and child with whom you come in contact."[28]

To put it simply, make sure that every time someone deals with you, they get more value than they put in. This applies to your clients as much as your staff.

In fact, after reading the passage above for the first time, I decided to change the way I lead my team meetings. That slight adjustment boosted sales by 250 percent and drastically decreased staff turnover. All I had done was offer mentorship to my employees. When my assistant was going through a stressful situation, I provided coaching and accountability. When my part-time contractors needed more work, I connected them with my network. When my video editor had a business idea, I helped him plan it out.

That is the kind of behavior that keeps your staff motivated and loyal. Couple that with good pay and a big goal to work toward, and you're guaranteed to develop a ton of positive and rewarding lifelong relationships.

Some skeptics who have challenged my leadership choices point out that if I let my staff work on their own business ideas, they would eventually leave my company. But that's a pure scarcity mindset. In this new job market, most employees will leave sooner or later anyway. If not because of their side businesses, it's because of a more suitable job elsewhere. What matters is that

---

[28] Wattles, *The Science of Getting Rich*, 128–29.

during the time they work with me, they are fully dialed in on our mission.

Automate Your Team with Software

Now that you've assembled a good team and are nurturing these relationships, let's take a deep dive into the operations side of the business. In fact, after years of coaching, I have realized that one of the most common shortcomings in companies that can't get past the launch phase was the CEO's inability to manage the increasing complexity of their systems. In other words, when a business grows, stuff gets very complicated.

Let's say you are a self-employed accountant with four clients. All you need to do is client work, admin work, and some basic marketing. That's pretty simple, right? But when you're scaling, you start dealing with staff meetings, webinars, new funnels, YouTube videos, podcasts, social media, customer service, a multitude of offers, and much more.

But that's not all. Each task mentioned above has its own set of subtasks, and sometimes subtasks also have their own subtasks. And to make matters worse, each subtask needs to be completed at a different time and by a different team member.

The result is a complex tree diagram that's ever evolving, and if left unchecked, it can cause the entire system to collapse. In the best-case scenario, your team forgets to upload a podcast episode, but in the worst, you may end up losing sales and clients.

To see how quickly things can get out of hand, take a look at figure 12, and notice how many tasks, subtasks, and deadlines are generated when you decide to launch just one new project, like a podcast.

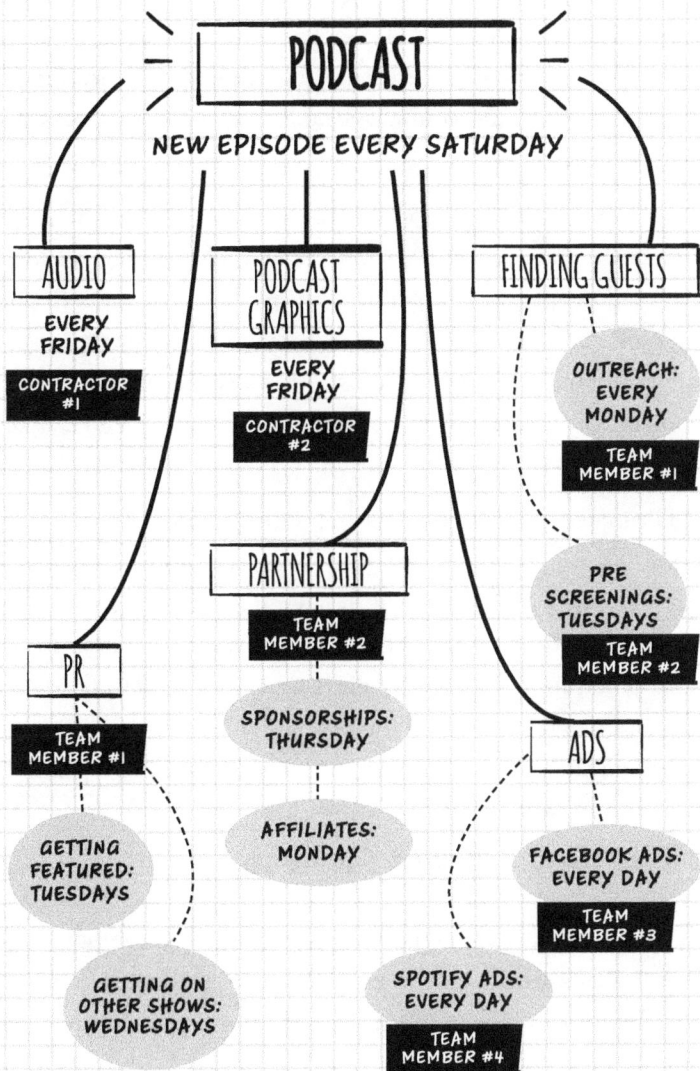

Figure 12: Launching a New Project

But this is not bad news. It just means that you need to use a team-productivity tool to keep track of all the moving parts. For example, at The Remote CEO, we use a fantastic tool called Todoist. This app allows me to create projects, list out all the tasks, create several layers of subtasks, assign each item to a team member, set due dates, and communicate by leaving notes, messages, and attachments.

Once you master a tool like Todoist, and your team uses it consistently, you are one step closer to automating your business. So instead of spending hours in meetings figuring out who does what, you can manage your entire company from an app. If you want to know more about Todoist, head over to the Partnership section on our website (www.denierob.com/partners), and get your free custom templates to get started.

Ultimately, there's no secret to building a good remote team. Sure, messaging apps and team-productivity tools will make your life easier, but it all boils down to having good people who work well together. If you were to build a Ferrari from scratch, for example, you'd need top-quality parts that do their jobs flawlessly. You wouldn't grab a random engine, four old wheels, and a broken chassis and then complain when it doesn't work like a Ferrari.

Building a Culture of Success

One of the most challenging feats when running a remote business is to maintain good communication across all team members. And when those touch points disappear, the culture vanishes with them.

For example, when I worked in corporate sales, we had a fun culture. Then one day we had to evacuate the building due to some major water damage, and the whole sales department worked from home for about 10 business days. Those turned out to be the worst two weeks for revenue and calls booked in the business's history.

The company had done everything in its power to set us up for success, or so they thought. They gave us phones, laptops, and an extra monitor. They let us bring home stationery, ergonomic chairs, and even desks for those who needed one. But they neglected the culture. Instead of having our morning pump-up meetings, we received an email from the manager. There were no side chats at the coffee machine, no lunch break games, no public recognition for the top sales reps. There was just you and your list of calls to make.

Fortunately, when the two weeks were over, we flocked back to the office, and things returned to normal. But for those businesses that always operate remotely, this is a critical point.

As Harvard Business Professor Tsedal Neeley explains in her book *Remote Work Revolution*, "For remote workers, team cohesion depends on two interrelated factors: the frequency of interactions with other team members, and the quality of relationships that these interactions form. More important than collocation is the extent to which people feel included in the group: whether they feel recognized, engaged, and up to date on the team's progress."[29]

So if you don't know where to start, let me give you a few ideas on how to use video calls to fast-track your company culture and build meaningful relationships.

- Get your team to work on group projects without you.

---

[29] Tsedal Neeley, *Remote Work Revolution: Succeeding from Anywhere* (New York: Harper Business, 2021).

- Schedule virtual lunches or virtual coffee breaks.

- Encourage people to suggest improvements to office systems.

- Promote nonwork-related talk right before and after meetings.

- Get more senior team members to check up on new hires.

- Recognize team members in front of their peers for their good work.

Add Your Team's Keystone

With all your systems in place, a cohesive team, and a strong company culture, you have reached the Promised Land of every lifestyle entrepreneur: you can hire an operations manager and truly put your business on autopilot. For example, my operations manager handles relationships with the social media manager, the designer, the web developer, the ad specialists, and the podcast editor. And since my assistant manages my email inbox and the relationships with all the podcast agencies and partners, my schedule tends to be pretty light.

Up to this point, I still had to show up multiple times every day to make sure work was getting done. But once I delegated the day-to-day management of my business to a professional with experience, I could work a lot less and enjoy the fruits of my hard work.

But this doesn't mean that I don't work anymore. As a coach, I'm still running my group calls and creating my own content. But because I batch those tasks on a specific day, aside from our morning huddles, I'm free to do whatever I want.

SECTION 5
LIFESTYLE DESIGN

CHAPTER 15

PLAN YOUR PERFECT LIFESTYLE

Start with Self-Care

Your own lifestyle is kind of a big deal in building your lifestyle business. The following chapters aim to help you design your environment, habits, and schedule to achieve maximum productivity, health, and well-being. The more you master these things and can take care of your mind and body, the faster and more robustly your business will grow.

So before you sacrifice your self-care routine and stop bonding with your loved ones in the name of getting more done, remind yourself that a happier you will work better and smarter.

Prioritizing self-care doesn't mean meditating as soon as you wake up or working out before breakfast. It means sticking to these habits even when you don't feel like it. My coach, Craig Ballantyne, calls these habits "non-negotiables."

In his book *The Perfect Week Formula*, he lists a few of his non-negotiables. Then he proceeds to say, "For me, these cornerstone non-negotiables make the hardest parts of achieving my goals 10× easier and reduce my need for willpower or motivation.

[...] If I consume my five servings of greens every day and 1.5 liters of water, I feel better, think better, and move better all day long. If I do my 10 minutes of meditation daily, I'm less likely to slip back into anxiety, avoid envious thoughts, and more likely to stay focused at work. These non-negotiables 'trickle down' and create a virtuous cycle that makes it easy to stick to my other positive habits without requiring Herculean mental effort."[30]

We'll cover a few simple self-care and fitness routines in the next chapter, but for now, here's my personal stack:

1. Brushing my teeth, trimming my beard, and moisturizing (10 minutes)

2. Drinking a cup of tea and reading 20 pages (60 minutes)

3. Listening to an audiobook, working out, and having a cold shower (20 minutes)

4. Meditating and stretching (20 minutes)

5. Drinking a big glass of water and taking my supplements (five minutes)

Some of these habits help me maintain the right mindset, while the others help me stay healthy and give me more energy.

Plan for Meaningful Work

And now that you're taking care of yourself, let's look at your work non-negotiables, remembering that not all work is created equal.

When I first started my agency, I worked around the clock, yet I was barely making enough money to pay my bills. That's

---

[30] Craig Ballantyne with Austin Gillis, *The Perfect Week Formula* (Denver: Early to Rise Publishing, 2019).

because I was only focusing on revolving tasks. I posted on social media, answered emails, and dealt with clients. But unfortunately, those were all upkeep tasks that were doing nothing to grow my business. I had created my own hamster wheel, and I was running on it.

Instead of doing that, think about your goals and identify your movers (go back to chapter 3 if you don't remember what they are).

For example, when I was scaling my agency, my movers were: running sales calls, getting referrals, gathering testimonials, and hiring good talent. But now that I am running my group coaching program and I have a big team helping me, my movers are writing this book, writing content for my blog, and coming up with good YouTube and Facebook ads.

Once you have a list of movers, it's time to plug them into your schedule along with your other non-negotiables. But before shoving hours of work in your calendar, let's be strategic about it.

If your movers require you to interact with other people (prospects, clients, or partners), you must match your schedule to theirs. But if they are like mine (mainly deep, concentrated work), find the quietest time of the day and reserve it for that.

When you run a remote business, your schedule may vary. My U.S. clients, for instance, are between six and nine hours behind my time zone, so on the day I have my group coaching call, I'm off from lunch until late evening, and I run the call from 11 p.m. to midnight. Then the morning after, I still wake up at 5 a.m. to get my meaningful work done, and then I have a nap around 9 a.m.

The key to getting ahead every day is to save your most important work for the very first part of your day. That way, you never fall behind with your movers.

But what about the rest of your day? In his best-selling book *Deep Work*, Cal Newport explains that we can only sustain deep concentration for three slots of about 90 minutes each. So, if you use your first slot early in the morning, you still have three hours left to produce meaningful work throughout the day.[31]

My goal is not to give you a strict timetable to follow. Instead, I want you to test a few schedules and stick to what works best for you. Then once you take care of your movers, you can set aside time for your reactive work, like meetings, emails, and other interactive tasks.

At this point, your schedule should look something like the one in figure 13.

[31] Cal Newport, *Deep Work: Rules for Focused Success in a Distracted World* (New York: Grand Central Publishing, 2016).

5 AM	Wake up/Coffee
	5:15 AM
	Writing (Book, Blog Posts, Newsletters)
6 AM	
7 AM	
8 AM	7:30 AM
	Self Care
9 AM	
10 AM	
11 AM	
Noon	
1 PM	1 PM
	Sales Calls
2 PM	
3 PM	
4 PM	

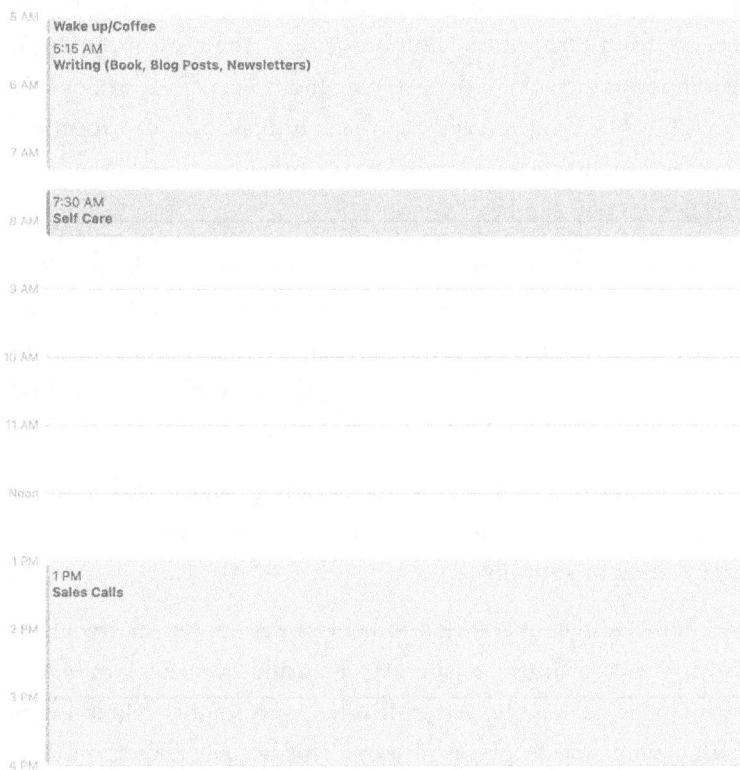

Figure 13: Your Schedule

Set Aside Time for Your Relationships

Now that your work is taken care of, it's time to make room for your relationships.

Ray Dalio often talks about the importance of cultivating meaningful relationships at work and in your personal life. In a tweet from December 2020, he writes, "The most meaningful relationships are achieved when you and others can speak openly to each other about everything that's important, learn together, and understand the need to hold each other accountable to be as excellent as you can be."[32]

That's why you must schedule these meaningful interactions in your calendar, primarily when you work remotely. Otherwise, you may take the path of least resistance and use all your free time watching YouTube videos or scrolling through social media. And as an introvert, I know a thing or two about that!

Before you can plug time for building meaningful relationships into your calendar, you need to figure out what the meaningful areas in your life are.

For example, in addition to being an entrepreneur, my client Lucas is also a fitness enthusiast. So, aside from his family and business associates, he has cultivated meaningful relationships with a couple of people at his gym. This way, he feels stimulated in all the key areas in his life.

And in my case, my wife and I recently had a baby daughter, so I mainly spend time outside work with them. But since I like to read and write, I have carved out two 30-minute slots a week

---

[32] Ray Dalio, "The most meaningful …," Twitter, December 14, 2021, https://twitter.com/RayDalio/status/1359155905254879245.

in my calendar to speak with two friends who share the same passion.

Let's pause again and look at figure 14 to see what your calendar should look like now.

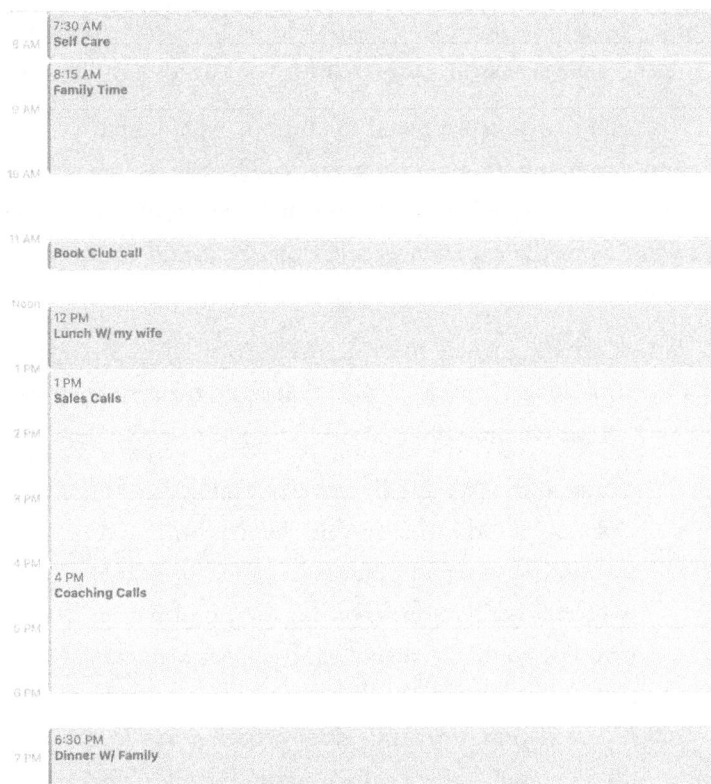

Figure 14: Your Schedule

Design Your Trips or Full Moves

So, you have accounted for all your activities, and it's time to decide whether you will stay local or travel while working. The beauty of running a remote business is that you don't have to commit to either one of the two options. In fact, for the first few years, my wife and I stayed in Toronto. Initially, I just worked from home. Then I rented an office in a shared space. And only when my wife started working remotely did we decide to move to Europe. Whether you are single, married, or have kids or not, you can set up your travels in a way that fits your needs and lifestyle.

The main reasons we opted for Europe were better weather, proximity to many travel destinations, and family. When it's your time to decide where (and if) you want to go, think about what you want from the experience, and don't be afraid to test a few locations.

When deciding where to work, three essential factors to consider are time zones, internet connections, and tax systems (if you choose to relocate abroad).

> Time zones: We briefly covered time zones in chapter 13 and earlier in this chapter. Still, I am mentioning it again because it should be one of your main criteria for choosing your destination if you perform any client-facing activities. For example, I only run live coaching calls once a week, so the 11 p.m. start time doesn't bother me. But if I had regular client calls at night, I wouldn't be happy about it because that would interfere with my early-morning routines.

> Internet connections: One of my agency clients owns a successful lifestyle e-commerce business, and he had decided to relocate to a small island in Thailand to create video content. When he arrived at this paradise, he was in awe, but that

lasted only a few minutes because he realized the island had a damaged broadband network and minimal cell service.

Tax systems: I can tell you from experience that you should always talk to your accountant if you plan to remain abroad for an extended time. But, if you decide to make a permanent (or semipermanent) move, don't let higher taxes prevent you from relocating, especially if we're talking about a marginal difference. My accountant put it beautifully when he said, "Sure, you may spend 10 percent more in taxes, but if the cost of living is lower, and the quality of life is much better, you are more than breaking even. You own a lifestyle business, after all."

Revisit Old Passions You Had Set Aside

And this takes me to the last question of this chapter: "What will you do with your free time?" After all, you worked so hard to free up your schedule. It would be such a waste if you just sat around all day.

In his best-selling book *The 4-Hour Work Week*, Timothy Ferriss talks about his activities before, during, and after he grew his business, from kickboxing in China to tango in Argentina and break dancing in Taiwan.[33] But you don't need to do all that. In fact, your best bet is to focus on one activity at a time.

For example, my client Andre focused on growing his

---

[33] Timothy Ferriss, *The 4-Hour Workweek: Escape 9–5, Live Anywhere, and Join the New Rich* (New York: Crown Publishers, 2007).

e-commerce business for years, but he always had a passion for collectibles. So when he was able to free up his schedule, he resumed his interest and started trading memorabilia. And since this happened shortly before the 2021 non-fungible token craze, he could capitalize on that and turn his passion into his primary business model.

But whether you are looking to monetize your additional interests or want to live a more fulfilling life, I recommend you dedicate a few years to each one of them and explore them fully.

True mastery of a craft takes time. In his best-selling book *Outliers*, Malcolm Gladwell talks about the 10,000-hour rule, and even though that's a rough estimate, you won't find true fulfillment in any activity unless you stick to it in the long run.[34]

Figure 15 shows a sample of how you could lay out a list of passion projects throughout a 25-year period.

---

[34] Malcolm Gladwell, *Outliers: The Story of Success* (Boston: Little, Brown and Company, 2008).

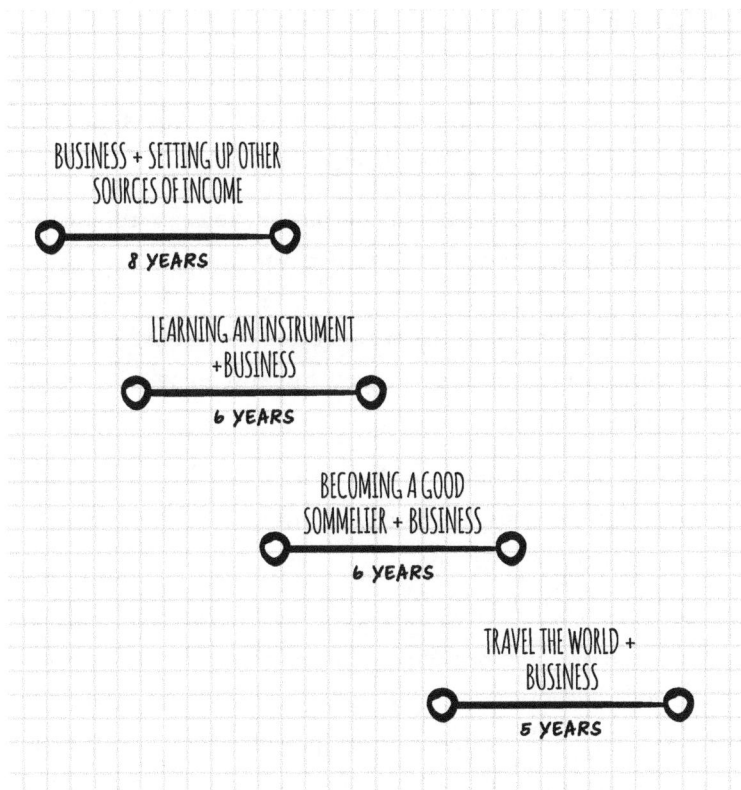

Figure 15: Passion Projects

Of course, that's assuming that your lifestyle business is not in growth mode and only keeps you busy for 15 to 20 hours a week. During the growing phases of your business, though, you should use your free time to recharge and spend time with your friends and loved ones. Like the Getting Things Done method creator, David Allen said, "You can do anything, but not everything."[35]

35 Keith H. Hammonds and David Allen, "You Can Do Anything—but Not Everything," *Fast Company*, April 30, 2000, https://www.fastcompany.com/40384/you-can-do-anything-not-everything.

Keep in mind two things:

- Whether or not mastery indeed requires 10,000 hours, if you practice something daily for four hours, you'll hit that milestone in less than seven years.

- When you undertake a new project, you can still use your downtime to do what you've already mastered.

In figure 13, for example, we allocated the last five-year block to traveling while working, but you can still enjoy wine tasting and music in your free time.

In case you're wondering, after spending eight years in music and 10 full-time years in business, I am now tackling my third stage: my passion for writing.

No matter what activities you choose to undertake, don't forget that you are now perfectly equipped to master them. You've scaled your business. You know how to perform deliberate practice, you are resilient, and you are patient. These are the only traits you need when learning a new skill, so keep expanding your horizons and have fun!

CHAPTER 16

FITNESS AND WELL-BEING

Work Out for Energy and Confidence

As a recovering couch potato, I knew I needed to be strategic with my fitness—but it took me a long time to realize I could transform my health by working out just 10 minutes a day.

After doing some research, I found many short fitness routines, and I decided to alternate between them during the week. I even incorporated a version of the 5BX or Five Basic Exercises. The Royal Canadian Air Force created this program in 1956, and Prince Philip swore by it to keep in shape for over half a century. So I thought, "If it's good enough for the Air Force, it's good enough for me."

If you're not looking to compete in a bodybuilding competition, alternating between some high-intensity training and weight lifting for just 10 minutes a day is more than enough. You'll look great, you'll be more confident during your sales calls and at your networking events, and you'll have enough energy to wake up early and do great, focused work all day.

Meditate for Focus and Stress Management

As you go about your day, new tasks and stimuli will pop up seemingly out of nowhere. And if you don't have an anchor to keep you grounded, you'll unintentionally drift away from your relaxed and productive state of mind.

If you're still on the fence, you don't have to believe me. But let me ask you, what do Arnold Schwarzenegger, Jennifer Aniston, Clint Eastwood, Katy Perry, David Letterman, Dr. Oz, Timothy Ferriss, 50 Cent, Steve Jobs, Arianna Huffington, Melinda Gates, Martin Scorsese, Oprah, Kobe Bryant, and Lady Gaga (among many others) have in common?

They've all claimed meditation is a crucial tool in their arsenal to achieve extraordinary results in their lives. To cite Ray Dalio, "Meditation, more than any other factor, has been the reason for what success I've had."[36]

So, sit down for just five minutes, close your eyes, and take a few deep breaths. And if you want to gamify the process as I did, get a wearable EEG device like the Muse headband. That way, you'll get instant feedback on how you're doing and a record of all your meditation sessions.

This short exercise will allow you to see past your mundane problems and will give you the clarity of mind to act with consistency, even when everything around you seems to be falling apart or chaotic. To understand this better, think about your

---

[36] Julia La Roche, "How Meditation Makes Ray Dalio Feel 'Like a Ninja in a Fight,'" Business Insider, February 12, 2014, https://www.businessinsider.com/ray-dalio-2014-2.

environment as the sea, and your mind as the captain of a ship. When the sea is calm, there's nothing to worry about. But when the storm comes, the captain needs to stay focused and work hard to keep the ship on course. Your mind is the same. Even though you feel in control on a normal day, you still need to strengthen your mind if you want to perform during stormy times.

Therapy for Mental Health and Happiness

Mental health is a sore topic for many because there's still some stigma around therapy. But I can confidently say that I wouldn't be where I am today without therapy—so much so that the first partnership I set up with The Remote CEO was with BetterHelp, the online portal that offers remote mental health services.

After my panic attacks and caffeine overdose, I was lost. The business was not growing, and every scenario I played in my head ended with me going bankrupt. I had just two small clients left, and my then-fiancée had had enough of me working 16-hour days. I was broke, I had crippling anxiety, and my doctor told me to "take it easy for a few weeks."

But even though I didn't have the budget for it, I knew I needed to take the leap and seek therapy. And right from the first session, I learned some extremely powerful tools to cope with my anxiety and negative thinking.

Sure, the average 45-minute session costs $100, but if you are willing to put your ego aside and deal with some hard truths, your investment will pay dividends for the rest of your life.

As for the time commitment, it's best to go at least once a week, especially at the beginning, so you don't hinder the discovery process. And since the point of therapy is to resolve problematic behaviors, thinking, and emotions, make sure to do the work between sessions.

There's a dark side to entrepreneurship that people don't like to talk about. Most mentors tell you to be persistent and optimistic until you see results.

But what happens when results don't come as fast as you would like them to? People often get discouraged and face depression, or they work around the clock and face burnout. An *Inc.* article from 2013 explains that "new entrepreneurs often make themselves less resilient by neglecting their health. They eat too much or too little. They don't get enough sleep. […] So it should come as little surprise that entrepreneurs experience more anxiety than employees."[37]

So, instead of waiting for the worst-case scenario, deal with your demons while they're still hatching. If you want to give BetterHelp a try, head over to the Partnership section of our website, denierob.com, and get your first month at a discount.

Being an entrepreneur means you're a lifelong learner, and nothing is more important than learning about yourself.

Eat Healthy for Energy and Performance

Like fitness, my eating habits had been poor for most of my adult life. I tended to overeat to cope with stress, and more often than not, I'd eat pizza or a cheeseburger for at least one of my daily meals. I'm ashamed to admit that I'm still tagged in a 2008 Facebook photo where my friend challenged me to eat three

---

[37] Jessica Bruder, "The Psychological Price of Entrepreneurship," *Inc.*, August 20, 2013, https://www.inc.com/magazine/201309/jessica-bruder/psychological-price-of-entrepreneurship.html.

McDonald's meals in one sitting. And I won.

When I finally had enough of dealing with acid reflux, brain fog, and dips in energy, I tried many diets—and failed at all of them. From low-carb to keto and paleo, they all got me pumped at the beginning, but once the excitement wore off, all I had left was a long list of foods I couldn't eat and a giant puzzle to solve: How do I stick to my diet when I'm on the road? That problem forced me to research an alternative route to achieving my goal, and within weeks, I had found the perfect regimen that I could follow for the long haul.

The first step was to look at my metrics and find out how many calories I burned in a day. Since I was living a pretty sedentary life, my Apple watch told me I was burning about 2,600 calories.

Then, for the first few days, I looked at the nutritional content of all the foods I was eating to make sure I wasn't ingesting more calories than I needed. (Pro tip—if you Google "____nutrition," you'll get data for almost any food you can think of.) By the end of the second week, I was estimating the correct portion sizes to lose weight and actually keep it off.

"But what about the quality of the food you eat?" you may ask. After all, best-selling author Dr. Jason Fung points out in his interview with Tom Bilyeu that "ice cream and salmon are not equally fattening for the same amount of calories."[38] To address that, I made sure to eat between one and two veggie servings each meal, I limited my intake of processed carbs, and to keep my gut healthy, I started eating one serving of plain yogurt or sauerkraut

---

[38] Tom Bilyeu, "The Biggest Mistakes People Make When Trying to Lose Weight | Dr. Jason Fung," May 6, 2021, YouTube video, 49:28, https://www.youtube.com/watch?v=XhPwjmbkgDs.

each day.

That was it! I didn't have to plan my meals or ask the restaurant staff for custom menu items. I also didn't feel deprived because I could eat anything I wanted as long as I hit the metrics I mentioned above at the end of my day.

I have been using this approach for five years, and it is incredibly liberating. As a result, I have plenty of energy and focus, and my body fat is consistently around 15 percent (which is in the "fitness" category, according to Healthline.com .)

Although this technique worked for me, I encourage you to speak to a dietitian if you are trying to make significant changes to your body composition. Your hormones and even the frequency at which you eat your meals will play a massive role in how your body processes food.

Sleep Well for Mental Health and Energy

The last puzzle piece to optimize your body and mind is sleep. I won't get into how bad my sleeping patterns were, though I'll remind you that I was a DJ for almost a decade. But once I decided to get eight hours of shut-eye a night, I had to face a hard truth: not all sleep is good-quality sleep.

See, I thought all I needed to do was sleep more. So instead of going to bed earlier, I just woke up at 10 a.m. But in the morning, I still felt groggy. In fact, best-selling author and health and fitness expert Shawn Stevenson explains this in his book *Sleep Smarter*.[39] To quote one of his blog posts, "It's been shown that humans get the most significant hormonal secretions and recovery

---

[39] Shawn Stevenson, *Sleep Smarter: 21 Essential Strategies to Sleep Your Way to a Better Body, Better Health, and Bigger Success* (Emmaus: Rodale, 2016).

by sleeping during the hours of 10 p.m. and 2 a.m. This is what I call 'Money Time.' "[40] By going to bed at 2 a.m., I had been completely missing out on rejuvenating sleep for months.

But like many good habits, going to bed early and waking up early is a hard one to form, especially when you are your own boss, and you work from home. But eventually, using James Clear's habit-forming framework,[41] I successfully transitioned to a consistent 10 p.m. to 5 a.m. sleep routine. Let's look at how I did it and how you can do the same.

> Obvious: I set a get-ready-for-bed alarm at 9:30 p.m. We recently set up smart lighting, too, so our living room lights go dim at that time.

> Attractive: 15 minutes before falling asleep, I meditate and drink herbal tea in bed.

> Easy: I eliminate distractions. The only tech gadget I can bring in my room is my watch. I keep my bedroom for sleeping, so my mind gets the cue when I walk in.

> Satisfying: When I practice gratitude in the morning, I'm always grateful for how well-rested and productive I am at 5 a.m.

But what if, like me, you tend to work late at night? Try testing the early-morning time slot instead. My night owl clients want to work after midnight because there's little noise and everyone is in bed. But doesn't the same apply at 5 or 6 a.m.? And in addition to the peace and silence, when you work in the morning, you get

---

[40] Shawn Stevenson, "Sleep Problems? 21 Tips to Get the Best Sleep Ever," *The Model Health Show* (blog), May 7, 2013, https://themodelhealthshow.com/sleep-problems-tips/.

[41] James Clear, *Atomic Habits: An Easy & Proven Way to Build Good Habits & Break Bad Ones* (New York: Avery Publishing, 2018).

clarity of mind after a restful night's sleep.

In fact, at the end of a long day, your subconscious mind knows that it's just trying to catch up with the day's work. Whereas in the morning, you feel totally in control of your time, and that extra confidence makes a big difference.

CHAPTER 17

THE SUCCESS BLUEPRINT AND THE TOOLBOX

Now you have all the necessary tools to build and scale your lifestyle business. But since we covered quite a lot of information, I will lay it all out one last time to give you the ultimate blueprint. On top of that, I also added a "toolbox" section to this chapter where I listed out all the tools my clients and I use to optimize our workflow, our environments, and our health.

Mindset

Before you put this book down for good, ask yourself if you already are the version of yourself that deserves the success you're going after.

If the answer is "No, I am not there yet," that's great! Keep on reading this book, and through spaced repetition, you will continue to replace your old limiting habits with new empowering ones.

But if you answered "Yes, I am that version of myself already," you may need a paradigm adjustment more than anyone else, or in other words, you need to revisit your belief system and your self-image. Personal growth is a never-ending process, and if you believe you've completed your self-discovery, I'm here to tell you that you haven't grasped the essence of it yet. I've come a long way as a person and as a business owner, but I'm far from being done with improving my paradigm. So I hope you'll join me in this continuous journey in the pursuit of greatness.

Brand Recognition and Reputation

Over the years I've had many clients from my marketing agency who chose to rely exclusively on paid ads to build a profitable business. And while they got some results, they were far from achieving true financial success.

Paid ads are like a megaphone; they grab attention and get you exposure, but they don't build ongoing trust and connection. However, these two factors are just as essential to get the sale.

Building your reputation online is the prerequisite for running profitable campaigns and ensuring lasting success for your business. So before spending thousands of dollars on ads, make sure your brand stands out.

In his best-selling book *One Million Followers*, Brendan Kane explains how online brand reputation is becoming a critical factor, even in Silicon Valley. "According to a Wharton business school study, social media popularity can demonstrate a start-up's ability to build its brand, integrate consumer feedback, and attract specific customer groups. Therefore, some investors take it into account when deciding what they will invest in."[42]

He goes on to describe his personal experience with building his brand on social media. "Since my numbers have increased, I've been able to leverage the influence for my own business—I've been able to secure more clients and partnerships. I was flown to Sweden to speak and run workshops at the IKEA global head-quarters; and I've secured speaking opportunities at events such as Web Summit in Portugal, the largest tech conference in the world with 70,000 attendees and speakers such as Al Gore, Elon Musk, Bono, Werner Vogels (chief technology officer and vice president of Amazon), and Dustin Moskovitz (cofounder of Facebook)."[43]

In short, if you take the time to build your brand with PR, social media, and even a book before running paid ads to your offer, you'll be miles ahead of those competitors who just want to buy their way to success.

Sales and Lead Generation

Your next focus should be on driving traffic to your offer and getting sales.

If you are selling a low-ticket item, you can automate the entire process with paid ads or influencer marketing by sending traffic to a sales funnel with great copy, images, and lots of social proof.

But if you are selling anything close to $1,000 or more, your sales process should focus on three steps: lead generation, booking calls, and closing the deal.

---

[42] Brendan Kane, *One Million Followers: How I Built a Massive Social Following in 30 Days* (Dallas: BenBella Books, 2018), 12.

[43] Kane, *One Million Followers*, 12.

In chapter 10, I showed you how to shortcut the lead-generation process by using Sales Navigator on LinkedIn. But doing outreach on Instagram or other social platforms is almost as convenient when you use hashtags to search your prospects.

If you are selling to a well-defined business-to-business audience, you can pay someone to compile lead lists from business directories and then reach out with cold emails and cold calls. Keep in mind, though, that this method won't allow you to leverage the brand status you built on your social media profiles.

Once you start conversations with your leads, your goal is not to sell right away. Instead, foster relationships by asking questions to find out how you can help your prospects. And to build trust, offer them an e-book or free training in exchange for their email addresses.

If you are doing this at scale, put together a direct-message sequence that your team can use on your behalf. That way, you only have to step in when your prospects ask very specific questions.

Once you or your team book a sales call, it's time to focus on closing the deal. We talked about how many calls this should take and how you can maximize the number of deals that close on the spot. We also looked at a simple way to control your energy and tone during the call to sound confident and in control.

And make sure you lead by example and get on some calls yourself before delegating to your team. Handling your sales process firsthand does two crucial things. First, it provides you with a bird's-eye view of what your prospects like (and don't like) about your offer, and it also gives you the confidence and insight to train your salespeople when you do delegate.

Team-Building

Once sales start pouring in, plan out your team, hire great staff members, and manage them effectively.

Planning how your team is going to look is an art. There are many ways you could go about it, so it's up to you (the CEO) to decide what roles to hire for, what types of contracts to set up, and how to get the different positions to work with each other.

When building your team, first decide what you want your schedule to look like. That's why we discussed the importance of assigning a monetary value to your time and using that as a threshold to decide what to outsource.

It's always a good idea to test your management skills when there's not too much at stake. So in the early stages of your business, feel free to hire a couple of extra contractors, and don't worry about making a few mistakes.

Then it's time to hire your team. We discussed how to avoid spending days sifting through hundreds of résumés. The goal is not to attract as many people as possible—all you need are 10 to 20 applicants who are truly a good fit for the position.

Most solopreneurs "hire fast and fire slow" to avoid doing the extra work of looking for and training a new person. That is entirely backward, and if you want your business to excel, you need to be picky with whom you choose to work. Remember that the quality of a company is a reflection of the quality of its parts.

So run multiple interviews and use psychometric assessments to match the right person to a precise and well-written job description. It will take some time to get it right, but managing the culture and operations of your business will be a lot easier once you do.

In fact, when you hire people who thrive in a remote-work environment, you can easily manage your team with productivity software and a few short meetings throughout the week.

But no matter who you work with, don't forget to offer more value than you take. People innately look for growth: more money, better health, knowledge, experiences, and better relationships. So, when you share your success with your team in the form of more money, knowledge, mentoring, and opportunities, you create an instant bond between your staff and the business.

Lifestyle Design

And finally, we looked at how to plan, create, and manage your perfect lifestyle. The big misconception among new lifestyle entrepreneurs is that everything will fall into place as long as you have lots of free time. But it's generally the complete opposite. The more free time you have, the less structure you tend to give yourself. So if you don't take control of your days, your mental and physical health will deteriorate.

The psychologist who first described "flow," Mihaly Csikszentmihalyi, wrote in the eponymous best-selling book that "ironically, jobs are actually easier to enjoy than free time, because like flow activities they have built-in goals, feedback, rules and challenges, all of which encourage one to become involved in one's work, to concentrate and lose oneself in it. Free time, on the other hand, is unstructured, and requires much greater effort to be shaped into something that can be enjoyed."[44]

---

[44] Mihaly Csikszentmihalyi, *Flow: The Psychology of Optimal Experience* (New York: Harper and Row, 1990), 162–63.

When I first read this inspiring paragraph, I realized that the antidote to boredom and lack of fulfillment is neither more free time nor more work but the structure itself. So, set personal goals and work on them daily. Whether you want to lose weight, learn a new language, or become a better partner, you can turn any idea into a structured project that you can pursue and have fun with while doing it.

The goal is to treat your free time with the same passion and structure you employ in your business. Don't snooze your morning alarm, just as you wouldn't snooze an important meeting. Don't skip your meditation session, just as you wouldn't skip a sales call. Don't let people talk you out of your plan to travel the world, just as you wouldn't let them talk you out of starting a business.

That's the most challenging part of being a lifestyle entrepreneur. Sticking to your personal activity schedule even when it "doesn't matter" is the only way to scale to millions while living the lifestyle of your dreams. But only when you reach that level of respect for your leisure time will you be able to juggle high levels of responsibility with the gift of nearly unlimited time off.

The Toolbox

This section will give you additional tools and tips to hold yourself accountable and be consistent with your productivity. It is intended as a guide, so although you can read the following pages from top to bottom, bookmark it and refer to it anytime you need to optimize your environment.

Eliminate Distractions Online and in Real Life

1. **Block social media from your computer:** News Feed Eradicator for Chrome will block the feeds of the most popular social media platforms, including Facebook, Instagram, LinkedIn, Twitter, and Reddit.

2. **Eliminate other distractions on your computer:** Set up tab presets on your browser so that only the tabs you need will open up when you launch your browser. For example, when I launch Chrome, I automatically get my blogging tool and my Todoist app.

3. **Block apps on your smartphone:** Set up Downtime on an iOS device or get a third-party app like Freedom to block selected apps from your device. (It works with android as well.)

4. **Eliminate distracting noises 1:** Invest in good noise-canceling headphones like the Bose QuietComfort or the Sony WH-1000XM3.

5. **Eliminate distracting noises 2:** I stumbled upon a white noise machine when we used it for our newborn, and it was life changing. Placing the white noise machine between you and the source of the distraction will isolate you from that sound.

6. **Eliminate distracting noises 3:** Use earplugs. I use them in bed every night, but I also use them during some deep-work sessions to block out background noise.

7. **Eliminate distracting visual cues 1:** Put your phone in Airplane Mode or Do Not Disturb to avoid seeing notifications on your home screen.

8. **Eliminate distracting visual cues 2:** If you are like me,

and you find yourself picking up your phone when you shouldn't, put it high up in a closet in another room. The harder it is to grab, the better. When I do that, I forget about it for hours.

9. **Eliminate distracting visual cues 3:** If you like watching TV or playing video games, hide your remote and game controllers the way I described above.

10. **Eliminate the need for your mobile device:** Get a smart speaker like a Homepod to control your devices and your ambiance with your voice. I use it to change the lighting, listen to music, send messages, set work reminders, and more.

11. **Systematize your passwords:** Use a password management tool like LastPass to save time logging in from different devices. Plus, you can grant access to specific sites to your team members without sharing the passwords with them.

Stick to Fitness, Diet, and Self-Care Routines

1. **Stick to a healthy diet 1:** Set up premade-meal deliveries, and put your diet on autopilot. Most companies deliver on a Sunday or a Monday, so you have healthy and delicious meals for the whole week.

2. **Stick to a healthy diet 2:** Order meal kits with recipes. This is great for two or more people. My wife and I have been using HelloFresh for months, and since we enjoy cooking, it makes eating healthy fun and manageable.

3. **Stick to a healthy diet 3:** Get your groceries delivered. Come up with a meal plan and set three alternatives for

each dinner. That way, you keep things interesting, but planning is much easier.

4. **Stand up:** Get a stand-up desk and make sure you also get a memory foam matt to stand on to avoid joint and back pain. I try to move my legs often at my stand-up desk, doing calf raises and small squats to activate my muscles.

5. **Walk 1:** Get a treadmill desk. Instead of buying a treadmill desk, I already had two stand-up desks, so I simply put a treadmill under one of them. I walk about five to 10 miles a day on it.

6. **Walk 2:** Get a smartwatch or a pedometer if you don't already have one. By gamifying your exercise, you'll get more done, and you'll stick to it. For example, I don't go to bed unless I've walked 10,000 steps that day.

7. **Meditate 1**: Invest in a Muse headband. This EEG device will give you instant feedback on how you meditate and will keep a record of your sessions. The newer models also monitor sleep.

8. **Meditate 2:** To spice things up, get a membership at a flotation tank center. Sensory deprivation (or flotation) tanks are great for stress relief, better sleep, and more.

9. **Sleep better 1:** Use earplugs. My sleep has been light for quite a while, so I use earplugs to make sure I don't wake up in the night.

10. **Sleep better 2:** Get blackout curtains. If any light comes in from the window at night, you are not getting the best sleep you can.

11. **Sleep better 3:** Keep your bedroom temperature at

around 65°F or 18.3°C. Your body temperature drops during sleep, so if your room is too warm, instead of resting, your body will be busy trying to lower its core temperature.

12. **Work out 1:** If you can't justify joining a gym, buy and keep your workout gear in a very obvious place in your home and set a daily 10-minute workout goal.

13. **Work out 2:** Use an app like The Fitness App by Jillian Michaels, where you can find all sorts of workouts, some of which are as short as seven minutes. The goal is to show up every day (except rest days)—even if it's just for seven minutes.

14. **Work out 3:** Invest in a VR set and use an app like Fit XR to take high-intensity interval training, boxing, or dance classes. For example, I use Fit XR for boxing, and I am totally exhausted after their workouts.

15. **Self-care 1:** Buy some bath salts and get in the habit of taking a hot bath every couple of days. It helps with muscle pain, blood pressure, mood, and more. If you don't have access to a sauna, a hot bath is the next best thing.

16. **Self-care 2:** Have a cold shower! I know it's the opposite of a hot bath, but it lowers inflammation, promotes heart health, boosts energy, and increases confidence. And it does all this in less than three minutes. So try it out after your hot bath—I'm serious!

17. **Self-care 3:** Read instead of watching TV. Your library should be much bigger than your TV set. We have books in every room in the house, while our TV is tiny and can only play Netflix.

Automate Your To-Do List

1. Don't use your willpower and memory to keep track of what you need to do next, especially when it comes to your daily routines. I set up recurring tasks on Todoist to ensure I never miss my daily, weekly, and monthly revolving tasks. Here are a few of them from my personal list.

Daily Routines

1. **Morning supplements:** I take omega-3 salmon oil, Vitamin D_3, lion's mane, alpha-GPC, and some amino acids. I am not a doctor, and this is not health advice, so speak to a specialist if you want to start taking supplements.

2. **Morning goal reading:** I read my vision and goals out loud every morning to make sure my head is always in the same mindset every day.

3. **Morning gratitude:** I list out five to 10 things I am grateful for every morning to shut the door on negative thinking and a scarcity mindset.

4. **Various house chores:** Although we have a cleaner coming twice a week, we still have to care for our baby, our two cats, and do other small tasks.

5. **Evening planning session:** I never finish my day until I've planned for the following one. This helps me stay in control of my time.

Weekly Routines

1. **Quality time with my daughter:** Every week I schedule four activities outside the house with my daughter.

2. **Weekly recap:** Every Sunday morning I look at how I did the previous week, and I plan the following one.

3. **Email a question to my coach:** Every Monday I write a question to my coach. If I can't think of one, I take the time to dig deeper until I find something.

4. **Go for a long walk in nature:** Every Saturday, I take a walk in the forest and "get lost" in nature. In Japan, this is called *shinrin-yoku*, or forest bathing.

5. **Visit family or video call them for an hour:** Every Sunday, we spend time with our families, and if we can't meet them in person, we meet online to catch up.

6. **Go over life and money goals with my wife:** Every second Thursday, my wife and I go over our finances, our work plans, and our family goals to make sure we stay on track.

Monthly Routines

1. **Get a haircut and massage:** On the first Tuesday of every month, I reset my hairstyle and body.

2. **Buy two items of clothing and get rid of two I no longer wear:** Every first Monday of the month I donate a couple of items and purchase something else to keep my wardrobe fresh for content creation and social events, such as hosting a big dinner with family and friends. We like to organize get-togethers at our house, so we make

sure to schedule them in regularly.

Miscellaneous

1. **Achieve flow faster:** Make a list of your important activities and designate a physical space for each of them. For example, I have a reading chair, a writing desk, a workout area, and a meditation spot, so my brain can switch to the correct mode faster.

2. **Manage cravings:** Buy a timer lockbox like the kSafe to eliminate temptations. If you find yourself eating too many cookies, playing video games, or trying to quit a bad habit, lock the items in the box for hours or even days.

3. **Wake up faster without coffee:** Get a HappyLight, especially for the winter. Light-therapy lamps mimic sunlight to help you manage your energy, focus, mood, and wake and sleep cycles, all without UV rays—or caffeine.

4. **Be accountable 1:** Tell someone whom you don't want to disappoint about your goals and deadlines, and get them to hold you accountable for them.

5. **Be accountable 2:** Make a bet with someone that you will finish a project on a tight deadline, and if you miss it, you'll have to give them $1,000. For example, I made a bet with my wife that I'd write this book in 30 days. I'm currently winning. Sorry, Brianne!

6. **Be accountable 3:** Set up a postdated payment of $1,000 to an organization that you hate, and only allow yourself to cancel it once you have completed your project. But, of course, get someone to hold you to it.

7. **Be accountable 4:** When working on a big project, pay for and schedule the next steps. For example, if you're building an online course, prepay your marketers, and prepare them to start working on the ads by the end of the month.

8. **Be accountable 5:** Go on social media and tell your entire network about your goal and tell them to follow up with you after the deadline to see the results of your hard work.

9. **Be accountable 6:** Invest in a coach. A coach can help you get accountability, check your blind spots, expand your network, and will show you the fastest way to go from where you are now to where you want to be.

CONCLUSION

Let's Go!

As the great Stoic philosopher, Epictetus, said in his *Discourses*, "The chief task in life is simply this: to identify and separate matters so that I can say clearly to myself which are externals not under my control, and which have to do with the choices I actually control. Where then do I look for good and evil? Not to uncontrollable externals, but within myself to the choices that are my own ..."[45] In other words, understand what you can control and what you can't. Then, only focus your energy and efforts on what's within your control, take responsibility for it, and learn to accept the rest.

If you hate your job but still need the money, save up for a few months, and go all-in with your side hustle. If you live somewhere you don't like, make a detailed plan of where, when, and how you will move, then execute it. If you are already running a business, but you are working around the clock, take ownership of your situation and optimize each process one by one. You can't control the weather, the economy, or the geopolitical situation, but you

---

[45] Epictetus, *Discourses*, trans. George Long (New York: D. Appleton and Company, 1904), 104.

can control how you react to them.

My wife went to a university for four years to study broadcast communication. And the same year she graduated, most major TV networks stopped hiring full-time reporters and anchors. But instead of fighting against an invisible enemy, she decided to look for a job where she could use her communication skills, and that's when she got into sales.

Brianne knew that the only thing she could control was her sales skills, so she practiced daily, and within nine months of graduating, she was already making a six-figure salary. And while she was advancing her career, many of her university friends were still jobless and complaining about the lack of opportunities.

The three little pigs had it all wrong. A sturdier house just doesn't cut it anymore. Build a big boat instead. The key to success is to adapt to ever-changing circumstances and stay afloat. As long as you can evolve fast enough, you'll always uncover a new opportunity.

If you made it to the end of this book, you are already an outlier. As wealth coach John Kanary said, "Excellence is a commitment to completion,"[46] so you are on the right track. But now it's time to apply the same drive and mentality to your very own lifestyle business.

It's not going to be easy or happen quickly, but I'll let you in on a secret. Being successful is easier than settling for a life you don't want. In fact, whether you chase your dreams or sit on the sidelines, you still have to put in the hours. You'll still have to show up to work even if you choose to live a mediocre life. You

[46] Proctor Gallagher Institute, "You Were Born Rich • Full Seminar [Remastered]," last updated October 23, 2019, YouTube video, https://www.youtube.com/playlist?list=PLVuv8qtX5I89dRY3YYpzGv22fyF4qCfZB.

may have to wake up early, sit in traffic, deal with poor-quality clients, worry about bills, settle for a smaller home, or give up on your dream vacation. But on top of all that, you'll also have to deal with a terrible emotional burden called regret.

So instead of choosing the path of least resistance today, embark on this journey with us and secure a lifetime of wealth and freedom for yourself and those you love.

BIBLIOGRAPHY

Amazon Staff. "2016 Letter to Amazon Shareholders," Company News. April 17, 2017. https://www.aboutamazon.com/news/company-news/2016-letter-to-shareholders.

APB Speakers. "Atomic Habits: How to Get 1% Better Every Day—James Clear," August 7, 2018. YouTube video, 8:03. https://www.youtube.com/watch?v=U_nzqnXWvSo.

Ballantyne, Craig, and Austin Gillis. *The Perfect Week Formula*. Denver: Early to Rise Publishing, 2019.

Bilyeu, Tom. "The Biggest Mistakes People Make When Trying To Lose Weight! | Dr. Jason Fung," May 6, 2021. YouTube video, 49:28. https://www.youtube.com/watch?v=XhPwjmbkgDs.

Bruder, Jessica. "The Psychological Price of Entrepreneurship." *Inc.*, August 20, 2013. https://www.inc.com/magazine/201309/jessica-bruder/psychological-price-of-entrepreneurship.html.

Brunson, Russell. *Expert Secrets*. Carlsbad: Hay House, 2020.

Cardone, Grant. *Sell or Be Sold: How to Get Your Way in Business and in Life*. Austin: Greenleaf Book Group Press, 2012.

Chandler, Stephanie. "How Long Should Your Nonfiction Manuscript Be?" Nonfiction Authors Association. April 7, 2014. https://nonfictionauthorsassociation.com/how-long-should-your-nonfiction-manuscript-be/.

Clear, James. *Atomic Habits: An Easy & Proven Way to Build Good Habits & Break Bad Ones*. New York: Avery Publishing, 2018.

Csikszentmihalyi, Mihaly. *Flow: The Psychology of Optimal Experience*. New York: Harper and Row, 1990.

Cuban, Mark. *How to Win at the Sport of Business: If I Can Do It, You Can Do It*. New York: Diversion Books, 2011.

Dalio, Ray. "If I had to choose …" Twitter, April 21, 2021. https://twitter.com/RayDalio/status/1384946112386191363.

Dalio, Ray. "The most meaningful …" Twitter, December 14, 2021. https://twitter.com/RayDalio/status/1359155905254879245.

Ducker, Chris. *Virtual Freedom: How to Work with Virtual Staff to Buy More Time, Become More Productive, and Build Your Dream Business*. Dallas: BenBella Books, 2014.

Epictetus. *Discourses*. Translated by George Long. New York: D. Appleton and Company, 1904.

Ferriss, Timothy. *The 4-Hour Workweek: Escape 9–5, Live Anywhere, and Join the New Rich*. New York: Crown Publishing Group, 2007.

Finkel, David. "Entrepreneurs May Be Particularly Susceptible to Shiny Object Syndrome. Here's How to Cure It." *Inc.*, January 16, 2020. https://www.inc.com/david-finkel/entrepreneurs-may-be-particularly-susceptible-to-shiny-object-syndrome-heres-how-to-cure-it.html.

Gladwell, Malcolm. *Outliers: The Story of Success*. Boston: Little, Brown and Company, 2008.

Greathouse, John. "5 Time-Tested Success Tips from Amazon Founder Jeff Bezos." *Forbes*, April 30, 2013. https://www.

forbes.com/sites/johngreathouse/2013/04/30/5-time-tested-success-tips-from-amazon-founder-jeff-bezos/.

Hammonds, Keith H., and David Allen. "You Can Do Anything—but Not Everything." *Fast Company*, April 30, 2000. https://www.fastcompany.com/40384/you-can-do-anything-not-everything.

Heriot, Drew, dir. *The Secret.* Melbourne: Prime Time Productions, 2006.

Instagram. "Introducing Instagram Reels," August 5, 2020. https://about.instagram.com/blog/announcements/introducing-instagram-reels-announcement.

Kane, Brendan. *One Million Followers: How I Built a Massive Social Following in 30 Days.* Dallas: BenBella Books, 2018.

Karim, Fazida, Azeezat A. Oyewande, Lamis F. Abdalla, Reem Chaudhry Ehsanullah, and Safeera Khan. "Social Media Use and Its Connection to Mental Health: A Systematic Review." *Cureus* 12, no. 6 (June 15, 2020): e8627. https://doi.org/10.7759/cureus.8627.

La Roche, Julia. "How Meditation Makes Ray Dalio Feel 'Like a Ninja in a Fight.' " Business Insider. February 12, 2014. https://www.businessinsider.com/ray-dalio-2014-2.

Lebow, Sara. "Worldwide Ecommerce Continues Double-Digit Growth Following Pandemic Push to Online." Insider Intelligence. August 19, 2021. https://www.emarketer.com/content/worldwide-ecommerce-continues-double-digit-growth-following-pandemic-push-online.

Lexico. s.v. "Resilience," 2022. https://www.lexico.com/en/definition/resilience.

Maltz, Maxwell. *Zero-Resistance Selling.* New York: Prentice Hall Press, 1998.

Morse, John J., and Jay W. Lorsch. "Beyond Theory Y." *Harvard Business Review,* May 1970. https://hbr.org/1970/05/beyond-theory-y.

Neeley, Tsedal. *Remote Work Revolution: Succeeding from Anywhere.* New York: Harper Business, 2021.

Newport, Cal. *Deep Work: Rules for Focused Success in a Distracted World.* New York: Grand Central Publishing, 2016.

Powers, David Guy. *How to Say a Few Words.* New York: Doubleday, 1953.

Rapier, Graham. "Starbucks Gets Away with Expensive Coffee in the Morning—but It's Losing Out to Cheaper Competition in the Afternoons (SBUX)." Yahoo! Finance. June 27, 2018. https://finance.yahoo.com/news/starbucks-gets-away-expensive-coffee-203600805.html.

Simpson, Jon. "Finding Brand Success in The Digital World." *Forbes,* August 25, 2017. https://www.forbes.com/sites/forbesagencycouncil/2017/08/25/finding-brand-success-in-the-digital-world/.

Sinek, Simon. *Start with Why: How Great Leaders Inspire Everyone to Take Action.* New York: Penguin Group, 2009.

Spangler, Todd. "YouTube Shorts at One Year: What the Video Giant Has Learned About the 60-Second Format—and What's Next." *Variety,* October 15, 2021. https://variety.com/2021/digital/news/youtube-shorts-one-year-monetization-creator-fund-1235090053/.

Statista. "Coca-Cola Company: Ad Spend in the U.S. 2019,"

July 2020. https://www.statista.com/statistics/463084/coca-cola-ad-spend-usa/.

Stevenson, Shawn. "Sleep Problems? 21 Tips to Get the Best Sleep Ever." *The Model Health Show* (blog), May 7, 2013. https://themodelhealthshow.com/sleep-problems-tips/.

Stevenson, Shawn. *Sleep Smarter: 21 Essential Strategies to Sleep Your Way to a Better Body, Better Health, and Bigger Success.* Emmaus: Rodale, 2016.

University of Dundee. "Don't Make Major Decisions on an Empty Stomach, Research Suggests." September 16, 2019. https://www.dundee.ac.uk/stories/dont-make-major-decisions-empty-stomach-research-suggests.

Wattles, Wallace D. *The Science of Getting Rich.* Holyoke: Elizabeth Towne, 1910.